The Getaway Guide II

The Getaway Guide II

More Short Vacations in the Pacific Northwest

by Marni and Jake Rankin

Pacific Search Press

Pacific Search Press, 222 Dexter Avenue North,
    Seattle, WA 98109
© 1981 by Marni and Jake Rankin. All rights reserved
Printed in the United States of America

Designed by Judy Petry

All photographs are by the authors, except those on pages 13, 15, and 16,
    which are by Len Kellogg of 108 Ranch Resort

Cover: *Cape Perpetua Lookout*

Library of Congress Cataloging in Publication Data

Rankin, Marni.
    The getaway guide II.

    Bibliography: p.
    1. Hotels, taverns, etc.—Northwestern States—Directories. 2. Resorts—Northwestern
States—Directories. 3. Northwestern States—Description and travel—1951-   —Guide-
books. I. Rankin, Jake, joint author. II. title.
TX907.R323   647'.979   80-29486
ISBN 0-914718-56-8

Wherever you go and whatever you do in the outdoors, move at Nature's pace, seeking not to impose yourself but to lose yourself. If you must leave footprints, make them not with blindness but with care and awareness of the delicate balance around you. And if you must take souvenirs, take them not in your pockets but in your mind and spirit. In preservation lies the promise of renewal.

Pacific Search Press

Contents

Vacationing 1980s Style

Less than two years ago our first book, *The Getaway Guide,* was published as a guidebook for short, spur-of-the-moment vacations in the Northwest. It was based on the notion that brief getaways taken several times a year produce benefits far in excess of those to be gained from the traditional once-a-year variety.

Since then, some surprising things have happened that only increase the advantages of the short vacation close to home. One of these is the cost of air travel. Fares have skyrocketed to the point that for the price of coach fare to Hawaii, for example, two people can stay at the best resort in the Northwest for a full week—including all costs—and still save money. At the same time, the necessity to reduce gas consumption is now an accepted fact, and long automobile trips to far-off places have gone out of style. But taking a vacation now and then is still a necessary part of life, not just for the fun of it but also for the vital change of pace and new perspectives that our modern life-styles often shut out at the expense of our physical and mental well-being. In other words, the times have changed, but basic needs remain the same, and the result has been an upsurge of local travel and the popularity of the short vacation.

The Getaway Guide makes a start toward providing the information this new trend requires by cataloging the best-known and best-loved Northwest resorts that are open year-round and have facilities for a good variety of activities. But now, in *The Getaway Guide II,* we have sought to supplement that earlier work and meet the ever-growing demand for such information by describing vacation destinations of a different sort: those that are not so well advertised and not necessarily open all year but equal to the better-known getaways in enjoyment potential, which is what vacations are all about.

In selecting this new list of inns and resorts, we ranged once more across the Northwest, staying as guests ourselves at each new place to test its hospitality and quality of service. And in the process we were struck once again by the diversity of the Northwest and how only a few hours on the road or on a boat can transport you from broad ocean beaches to secluded islands to remote mountain glens to the dry, sunny clime of the Inland Empire. That makes the selection of a vacation destination a matter of mood. Do you feel like walking the beach, or breathing mountain air, or lounging in the sunshine? Do you want to be pampered and waited on in a full-service resort with every amenity or go somewhere rustic and secluded? Do you want rest and a chance to read or vigorous activity? Do you want to fish a stream full of trout or steelhead or ride a horse through the wilderness? The Northwest has them all; the nature of your getaway depends only on the choice you make.

Everyone, of course, has some favorite place that serves as a standard of comparison. Our objective in writing about these resorts has been to provide information that will enable readers to compare the atmosphere of each place, knowing what can be expected of it and what guests can do there, without being overwhelmed by detail.

The little attentions and niceties—such things as having fresh flowers in the room or a continental breakfast in bed—were also significant to us. We got into the habit of looking for these things and mentioning them because the operators thoughtful enough to do them tend to have an empathy for their guests that is usually reflected in other aspects of their operation as well.

Something we particularly enjoyed was the "American plan," which a number of these resorts have. Some or all meals are included in the basic tariff, and all of the guests convene for meals together at large tables, with dinner usually preceded by a cocktail period. We were delighted by the number of new friends we made and experiences we were able to share in conversations with people we would never have met under the usual system in which every couple eats in solitary splendor.

To make your getaway planning as simple as possible we've included two helpful lists at the back of the book: a checklist and a list of information sources. The checklist is a reminder of what you should do before leaving home and items you should pack to bring along with you, and the information sources list provides telephone numbers you can call to find out about such things as weather and highway conditions and ferry and airline schedules.

Every hideaway described in this book has become something special to us that we want to share. We enjoyed the research necessary to do the writing, but it is not finished, for it will be an ongoing project of updating as the getaway destinations and the people who run them change. And we will always be happy to hear from readers who have suggestions about places that should be added, deleted, or reassessed and rewritten the next time around.

North
Getaways

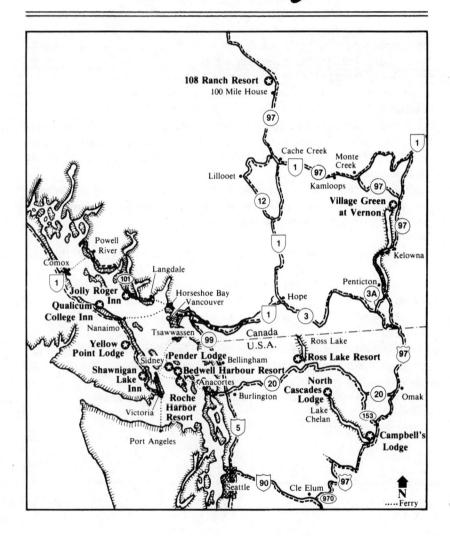

108 Ranch Resort
100 Mile House
97
Cache Creek
Monte Creek
Lillooet
1
97
Kamloops
12
Village Green at Vernon
97
1
Kelowna
Powell River
Langdale
Penticton
3A
Comox
1
101
Horseshoe Bay
Hope
Jolly Roger Inn
Vancouver
Qualicum College Inn
1
Nanaimo
Tsawwassen
3
Canada
U.S.A.
99
Ross Lake
Yellow Point Lodge
Sidney
Pender Lodge
Bellingham
Ross Lake Resort
97
Shawnigan Lake Inn
Bedwell Harbour Resort
Anacortes
20
North Cascades Lodge
20
Omak
Roche Harbor Resort
Burlington
153
Victoria
Lake Chelan
Campbell's Lodge
Port Angeles
5
90
Cle Elum
97
Seattle
970
N
.....Ferry

108 Ranch Resort

Distances:

From Seattle—385 miles; allow 8 hours

From Portland—560 miles; allow 12 hours

From Vancouver, B.C.—300 miles; allow 6 hours

Features:

Big, fully equipped resort with something to attract almost everybody; located in the heart of the vast Canadian Cariboo country where summers are hot, winters are cool, and both are dry

Activities:

Golf, tennis, horseback riding, fishing, and swimming in summer; cross-country skiing, ice-skating, curling, and snowmobiling in winter; saunas and hot spa

Seasons:

Year-round; outdoor summer activities are best May through October; skiing usually is good mid-December through February; early spring and late fall tend to be slack

Rates:

$35 to $40 for two people in a room; $50 in a housekeeping unit

Address:

Compartment 2, Rural Route 1, Hundred Mile House, B.C. V0K 2E0, Canada

Phone:

(604) 791-5211; toll free in Vancouver, B.C., 687-2334

Tennis courts at 108 Ranch flooded for skating in winter

British Columbia's Cariboo gained fame in 1858 when the discovery of yellow metal along the banks of the Fraser River precipitated a frantic gold rush. Thousands of miners and fortune seekers surged up the tortuous Fraser Canyon and fanned out into a vast, little known area bordered by great mountains and filled with never-ending forests and thousands of lakes and streams. Eventually, the gold seekers' main route led from the town of Lillooet in the south to the mines in Barkerville, east of Quesnel. The roads they pounded out over the years became known as the Cariboo Wagon Trail.

Today, British Columbia's Highway 97 closely follows the old trail, except that it starts at Hope instead of Lillooet and continues on past Quesnel north through the province, eventually merging with another famous road, the Alaska Highway.

The traveler is bound to notice, after leaving Hope, that the settlements become farther and farther apart and noticeably more functional. Pretty yards and architectural niceties disappear and the feeling that one is approaching frontier territory becomes stronger with every mile. It is thus quite a surprise to arrive at 108 Ranch in the center of the Cariboo and discover a resort as comfortable and up to date as any of the better known places to the south. Not only does it have all the usual amenities, but it also provides a wider range of outdoor activities than any but a handful of alternate vacation destinations.

Strikingly similar to the horse country of eastern Washington and

Oregon, the Cariboo terrain is hilly, pine tree country with sparse under-brush and a surrounding ring of mountains. The area's remoteness from moist, cloud-bearing ocean air enables it to boast more sunshine than Honolulu, resulting in summers that are ideal for riding and outdoor sports and dry, cold winters that provide the long-lasting, powdery snow favored by nordic skiers.

Routes and Distances

Part of the fun of a trip to 108 Ranch is the experience of getting there. After an easy drive from Seattle or Vancouver to the town of Hope, the highway takes you north across the Fraser River and into the precipitous Fraser Canyon. The nearly 100-mile drive along the brink of the gorge is spectacular, with continuous breathtaking sights of the river far below. It is impossible to follow this route without speculating about the formidable barrier it must have presented and the hardships that had to be overcome in the gold rush days when oxen, horses, and canoes were the only means of transportation.

On the old Cariboo Trail the custom was to designate way stations by their distance in miles from Lillooet. Official stops thus became "70 Mile House," "100 Mile House," or "150 Mile House." People who settled between these stations adopted the appropriate mileage for their own ad-dress, hence 108 Ranch or 115 Lodge.

To get to the ranch from Vancouver, take Trans-Canada Highway 1 through Hope to Cache Creek. There it joins B.C. 97, which continues north to 100 Mile House. Just eight miles farther on the left is 108 Ranch.

From Seattle or Portland drive Interstate 5 to Bellingham. On the north side of town look for the Guide Meridian Road (Washington 539) and follow it north until it intersects Route 546 just above Lynden. Take 546 to Sumas. At the customs house the Canadian inspector will want to know where you were born, where you are going, and whether you are packing any firearms (don't!). Then drive two miles to the intersection with the Trans-Canada Highway and proceed to Hope.

For pilots, the ranch maintains a fine, paved airstrip, conveniently located adjacent to the lodge.

Accommodations

The 108 Ranch Resort began ten years ago with 7,000 acres of what was formerly a 26,000-acre working cattle and horse ranch. The original lodge building was placed on a high rise of land where it could overlook a wide valley, now the golf course, and a tranquil lake to the west. Then several years ago, angled wings with additional rooms were added to each side of the main building in an orientation designed to provide each room with a good view.

Sixty rental units are now available, each with a spacious deck on the view side and an outside entrance convenient to parking. Most of the rooms are moderately priced. All are spacious and comfortably furnished, with either one queen-size or two double beds. The slightly more expensive units have kitchenettes and dining areas, and a few have full-scale kitchens.

Saunas and a whirlpool spa, both particularly welcome after a long day of skiing, are conveniently located on the lower level beneath the lobby.

Activities

The main part of 108 Ranch still is a working ranch, and, as might be expected, horseback riding is a major interest of many guests. The ranch maintains a long string of saddle horses, which makes it possible to suit every level of riding ability. Each day in summer guided trail rides are conducted, and in the evening hay rides are popular, as well as frequent barbecues, cookouts, and bonfire parties.

Numerous small lakes, well stocked with rainbow and eastern brook trout, are nearby; five of them are no more than fifteen minutes from the resort. More ambitious fishermen can take charter flights from the ranch's airstrip into otherwise inaccessible wilderness lakes that provide superb fishing experiences.

Summertime guests can also swim, play tennis, and golf. Finding such a fine golf course so far from any city is a real surprise. The P.G.A.

Recreation complex at 108 Ranch

approved course, with its 6,700-yard, eighteen-hole layout, is the site of several major Canadian tournaments. Guests of the ranch have unlimited use of the course for a fee, and the well-equipped pro shop provides rental equipment, carts, and lessons. The shop also is shared by a tennis professional, and five well-maintained Plexi-pave courts are available for the use

Guided trail ride to 108 Lake

of ranch guests. Swimmers and sunbathers have a choice of the outdoor pool in front of the lodge or a sandy beach on 108 Lake.

When winter comes to the Cariboo, cross-country skiing takes over as the predominant attraction. Because of rolling rangeland and winter sunshine, 108 Ranch has some of the finest skiing in Canada and is a favored spot for Canadian cross-country competition. Some forty miles of marked and groomed trails are maintained on ranch property, and thousands of unmarked acres can be explored on one's own. Three warming huts at strategic points along the trails provide good destinations at which to stop for a knapsack lunch. In winter, the golf-tennis shop is converted to a ski shop, with a cross-country instructor and all necessary rental equipment available.

The ranch has other winter activities besides skiing. Snowmobiles can be rented to explore the countryside and to take fast spins on the frozen lake, and the tennis courts are flooded for ice-skating and curling. After a day in the cold, the saunas and hot spa await, and following that, each evening between half-past five and half-past six a "Gluhwein" is held in the clubhouse, where hot spiced wine is served and a guitarist leads rollicking old-fashioned sing-alongs—making the evening, for many, the best part of the day.

Cross-country skiers on trails maintained by 108 Ranch

Dining

A large dining room is located above the pro shop in the clubhouse, just a short walk from the lodge. It provides the only food service available on the ranch, but it is open daily for all three meals.

This room, with its large picture windows allowing a 180-degree view of the valley and the lake and hills beyond, has a warm and friendly atmosphere. During warm weather, breakfast and barbecue dinners are often served informally at picnic tables arranged on the clubhouse patio below the dining room.

The dinner menu is not extensive, but it offers an adequate selection of steak and roast beef and usually includes a veal and a pork entree and a few seafood items. A dinner specialty also is announced each evening and is usually excellent. The wine list is a surprise to Americans, as it includes not a single selection from the United States. There are several Canadian wines, but most of the choices are moderately priced items from a variety of European countries—a good opportunity, actually, for a little experimentation!

As an alternative to the clubhouse dining room, there are two restaurants nearby. One is at the Red Coach Inn on the right side of the road on the northern outskirts of 100 Mile House. It is a conventional dining room with a pleasant atmosphere. In the opposite direction on the left side of the road is the decidedly unconventional Longbranch Inn, located at 115 Mile Lodge on Lac La Hache. It combines a lively neighborhood pub with a tiny dining room that serves delicious home-cooked meals. Each night there is a new choice of two or three entrées. Because of the limited seating, reservations are a necessity.

Qualicum College Inn

Distances:
From Seattle—183 miles, plus ferry; allow 6 hours
From Portland—330 miles, plus ferry; allow 9 hours
From Vancouver, B.C.—42 miles, plus ferry; allow 3 hours

Features:
Former prestigious boys' school with imposing buildings, now a stately resort hotel; located high on a bluff above the Strait of Georgia in an area famous for its wide beaches, warm water, and good summer weather; elegant dining facilities

Activities:
Visiting the beaches, bicycling, swimming, sauna and hot spa, nightly lounge entertainment; golf and tennis nearby

Seasons:
Year-round; July and August usually booked well in advance; 19 September to early June considered off-season

Rates:
$32 to $38 (Canadian currency) for two people in summer; $28 to $32 in off-season; economical package plans also available

Address:
Box 99, Qualicum Beach, B.C. V0R 2T0, Canada

Phone:
(604) 752-9262

Entrance to Qualicum College Inn

In spite of its name, the Qualicum College Inn will take you by surprise when you see it for the first time. Approaching from either direction along Qualicum Beach Road, you will pass through a maze of low-slung cabins and vacation houses dotted along miles of beach front. It is no wonder, then, that it is a bit of a jolt, albeit a pleasant one, to round a bend in the road and see, poised on the edge of a bluff, a stately old building looking very much like a baronial manor house from some time out of the past.

The history of the place reveals the reason for the architectural style and the even more unusual decor. It was built in the midthirties by a man of traditional taste as a private boarding school for boys, and during the long tenure of its founder it became an established British Columbian institution, educating students from around the world. The school's star did not fade until 1970 when it fell victim to inflation and the high cost of operation.

The building then changed hands and was completely renovated as an inn, which opened in 1972, with much of the decor, including photographs, trophies, and memorabilia, taken from the archives of the school. Other echoes of the past include the massive, dark furniture throughout the common rooms of the hotel. Truly medieval in design, the setting would probably make King Arthur and his knights feel at home. The chairs, for example, are so heavy that there is enough wood in one of them to make three ordinary chairs. This was the school's original furniture, sensibly created to withstand the onslaught of a continuous stream of exuberant youth.

Today the inn bustles with modern activity, but not enough to smother the lingering nostalgia and old-world atmosphere. Thus, although the inn is less than ten years old, it has an aura of history, tradition, and permanence that suggests it has been here for a long time and will continue for a long time to come.

Routes and Distances

For mainlanders, getting anywhere on Vancouver Island involves dealing with the intricacies of ferry boat schedules. Qualicum Beach is no exception. The most frequented way to get there is via the Nanaimo ferry from Horseshoe Bay in West Vancouver. Our time allowance of three hours from downtown Vancouver for this route assumes a half-hour wait at the ferry terminal. During much of the year this is a reasonable allowance, but during rush periods and in summer it may be necessary to arrive an hour or an hour and a half before sailing time. Call the ferry in advance (phone numbers are listed in "Information Sources") for advice about lead times.

When you get to Nanaimo, drive north on Trans-Canada 1 for

Wide expanse of beach at Qualicum

thirty-four miles. The highway does not pass through Qualicum Beach town, which is inland a short distance, but there is a standard sign on the highway designating the city limits. One mile beyond that, on the right, the Qualicum College Inn sign is prominently displayed. You can't miss it.

Accommodations

When the old school was converted to an inn, all the original rooms were modernized and redecorated, and a complete new wing was constructed. Rooms in the new wing are a bit larger than those in the original building and look out across the lawn to the strait. Typically, these rooms are furnished with two beds, a single and a double, a round card table, two lounge chairs, and a color television set. All the units on the lower floor have sliding glass doors that open directly onto the lawn. Prices of rooms in the new wing are on the upper end of the rate scale. Rooms in the older part are just as comfortable, although some are smaller and some face to the west, away from the strait. The rates accordingly fall on the lower end of the scale.

Activities

Without question, the overriding interest of guests at the inn is the beach, since the vast stretch of sands along the Qualicum waterfront is reputed to be one of the finest in Canada. For over a mile out to sea there is an extremely gradual gradient, allowing the sun to warm the shallow water to an unusually pleasant temperature compared with most saltwater beaches in the Northwest. As a result, the indoor pool at the inn does not draw much attention on warm summer days, although it is a pleasant diversion at other times of the year, as are the whirlpool spa and sauna housed in the same building.

The inn is fortunate to be flanked by golf courses. The lovely old Qualicum Golf Course, overlooking the Strait of Georgia, is one of the most scenic in Canada, and during a round on its nine holes it is no small task to keep an eye on the ball in the presence of such beauty. Just as close in the other direction is the new Eaglecrest Golf Club, a challenging par-seventy course, open to the public, with a driving range and practice green as well as a full pro shop facility. The club also boasts a good restaurant and lounge.

Although there are no tennis courts at the inn itself, three well-kept public courts are available in the Qualicum Village Centre, just a few blocks away and not difficult to find. The courts make a good destination for a bike ride, and both single and tandem bikes can be rented at the desk for a small fee. Many guests also enjoy bicycling on the quiet roads along the beach and exploring the area around the village.

The inn, by the way, is not directly on the beach, but occupies a high

Lawn at Qualicum College Inn overlooks Strait of Georgia

bluff, where it looks out across the strait to the mainland in the far distance. Those who do not want to take the walk (or drive) down can stay on the inn's lawn and enjoy the beach as a panorama. In the evening, to cap off the day, there is musical entertainment in the lounge, a good place to repair following dinner.

Dining

Perhaps more than anywhere else in the inn, the dining room, known as the Old Boys' Room, conjures up ghosts of the past. Its walls are covered with photographs of the school's cadet corps and rugby and cricket teams from years long gone by, and its heavy medieval furniture, upholstered in plush red velvet, is arranged under massive iron lanterns hanging from a high ceiling. Besides this unusual atmosphere, the inn unquestionably has one of the best kitchens north of Victoria. Even on weekday evenings it can be expected to be booked up, so advance reservations are always in order.

Good food, expertly prepared, is a matter of first priority with the management. The menu is extensive, starting with two full pages devoted to appetizers and salads. The most fascinating menu item—and one that befits the decor of the room—is the "Medieval Meal," which the chef will prepare for two or more people. If you order this feature of the house, the waiter starts by removing all of the silverware from your table (after all, they didn't use that in medieval times) and hanging a big bib around your neck. Then comes the food. The "First Remove" is soup, ladled from the cauldron and drunk from a cup. The "Second Remove" is a platter of seafood: ice-cold crab, prawns in the shell, raw oysters, and smoked salmon. A pair of nutcrackers is provided to crack the crab; otherwise, diners eat with their fingers. The "Third Remove" is another platter with an assortment of roast chicken, beef chunks, lamb, and pork strips. A hunting knife is provided to help with this. Not through yet, the waiter brings a "Fourth Remove" of mixed fresh fruit and finally the "Fifth Remove" of assorted cheeses on a wooden platter. It all adds up to a unique experience in dining.

Yellow Point Lodge

Distances:
> From Seattle—170 miles, plus ferry; allow 5½ hours
> From Portland—344 miles, plus ferry; allow 9 hours
> From Vancouver, B.C.—28 miles, plus 1¾ hour ferry ride; allow
>   2¾ hours

Features:
> Rustic accommodations, mild weather, lots of sunshine; strikingly
> unusual architecture and natural setting; all guests share a
> dramatic main room for tea and social contacts and eat
> together at common tables in a "country house-party" at-
> mosphere; adults-only resort—no children under sixteen and
> no pets

Activities:
> Fishing, clamming, oystering, beachcombing, tennis, golf, swim-
> ming, outdoor sauna and hot tub, sunbathing, volleyball,
> canoeing

Seasons:
> Year-round; summer season is always heavily booked

Rates:
> $78 to $94 for two people in a lodge room; $64 to $74 for two
> people in a cabin; includes all meals

Address:
> Rural Route 3, Ladysmith, B.C. V0R 2E0, Canada

Phone:
> (604) 245-7422

Entrance to Yellow Point Lodge

Anyone's first visit to Yellow Point is guaranteed to be a surprise and a delight. No matter how much you may have heard about it, Yellow Point will be different from what you have imagined. The long drive in from the road is tunnellike as it winds through a magnificent stand of old-growth fir and giant oaks and madronas. Then the inn comes into view, a massive log structure embraced by the branches of more great oaks. The entrance is approached over a single slab of natural rock that is nearly a half acre in size and slopes gently down from the inn door to the water's edge.

Once you step inside, you will have no doubt about the authenticity of the log structure. Everything is in massive scale, hand hewn in the old way. The exterior walls are logs sixteen to eighteen inches in diameter, ax-notched at the ends and chinked with oakum like a ship. The floorboards are polished fir three-by-twelves sawed on the site from native timber. The rafters are round poles of the traditional style, and the stone fireplace is nine feet wide and burns four-foot logs. Across from the fireplace two ancient madronas grow right through the floor and the roof; the structure was simply built around them.

The Yellow Point property encompasses 180 acres of forested land, including two miles of waterfront, with the point itself forming the apex. It got its name from a British Admiralty surveying party that noted how abundant bright yellow flowers on the rocks cause the point to stand out sharply as a landmark to ships in the channel.

The location, sheltered by Vancouver Island's mountainous spine and diagonally across from the mainland's famous "Sunshine Coast," boasts more sun and better weather than the Puget Sound area to the south.

Yellow Point today is more than just a lodge in a pretty forest on the water. It is now a venerable tradition, started by Jerry Hill, who as a young World War I veteran acquired this "useless piece of property" by homesteading and patiently built the lodge with his own hands. Today Jerry lives and thrives in the upstairs penthouse, and you may see him, with his big black dog, Ben, around the grounds; ask him to tell you the story, over an evening sherry, about the skull built into the fireplace and how it got there. Jerry continues to guide the resort's progress and has through the years held stoutly to a policy of preservation of old values and conservation of the land and its natural beauty. Now a "Friends of Yellow Point" society has been formed by people who love the place and consider it a natural landmark that must be preserved. They meet regularly and provide professional guidance to help the staff carry on the traditions Jerry Hill started.

Routes and Distances

Yellow Point lies between Nanaimo and Ladysmith on the east coast of Vancouver Island. To get there, take the Nanaimo ferry from Horseshoe Bay in West Vancouver. After landing at Nanaimo, go south on Trans-Canada 1 for three miles to Cedar Road. Follow it for several miles past Cedar to Yellow Point Road on the left. Signs direct you to the lodge, a total of fifteen miles from Nanaimo.

Those who come from the opposite direction, having taken the Tsawwassen ferry or the Washington State ferry from Anacortes to Sidney/Swartz Bay, must drive south to Victoria and then north to Ladysmith. Three miles beyond Ladysmith, look for the Yellow Point sign (at John's Service Station). Yellow Point is approximately six miles to the right.

From Portland the shortest route is via Port Angeles, where you board the Black Ball ferry *Coho.* See the chapter on Shawnigan Lake Inn for additional travel information.

Accommodations

Since all guests at Yellow Point are on the "American plan," in which the lodging rates include meals and recreational facilities, the only choice to be made is the type of lodging. There are basically two ways to go: the more comfortable is to stay in the cozy lodge itself where various accommodations are available, the other is to choose the more rustic—and less expensive—cabins scattered along the beach and in the

One of Yellow Point's beach cabins

nearby meadow.

All the lodge rooms, with their walls and ceilings paneled in cedar, reflect the authentic log construction of the building. The rooms are comfortably furnished, and the price range is based on whether the room has a bath, a shower, or only a washbasin. For the latter rooms, several communal baths are scattered down the hall. If the chance arises, try to book room 5. It has a balcony and a view out over the rocky finger of Yellow Point through a magnificent oak tree; it is a beautiful spot to relax.

The cabins are very different—they are absolutely basic. Some are separate one-room units, each with its own little porch, while others are strung together barracks-style with three or four rooms in a single building opening onto a common porch. Each cabin room of either type has a bed, a closet, and a little sheet-metal wood-burning stove to take the chill off the air. That is all. There is no running water, and centrally located community washrooms and showers must be shared. It is very much like camping out, except that a good bed, a roof overhead and a dramatic setting are ensured—and the price is right.

For those who would like to take children and pets on vacation it seems a shame they are not allowed at Yellow Point: it would be such a good place to romp and play. But because of the thin walls of the cabins, the shared bathing facilities, and the communal dining that adults find so

Sunny glassed-in porch at Yellow Point Lodge

enjoyable among adult company, they are reluctantly banned.

Activities

Two good asphalt tennis courts lie hidden in a grove of tall firs a short distance from the lodge. The only distraction we encountered during a game on these quiet courts was an eagle swooping overhead to land in the dead top of the tallest tree. We watched him and he watched us for the rest of the game.

Other active sports at Yellow Point are volleyball on one of the lawns, swimming and diving in the big saltwater tide pool, jogging and walking on the many wide trails through the forest, paddling a canoe or rowboat in the strait, or playing Ping-Pong in the solarium. Golfers can use two good public links in Duncan and Lake Cowichan not far away.

When the sun shines, the expanse of flat rock in front of the lodge is fine for sunbathing. A pile of canvas pads is kept handy under the eaves for people who want something to lie on, and there are a number of nooks and crannies in the rock to provide a little privacy.

Of course, exploring the beach is, as always on the waterfront, the number one activity. The rocky shore is full of tide pools and little sandy caves. There is an abundance of oysters to be picked and clams to be dug (the lodge kitchen will prepare your catch), and salmon run offshore. Moreover, Vancouver Island is known for its many steelhead streams, a number of which are close to Yellow Point, making it a convenient headquarters for fishermen during the season.

For some evening fun, ask at the desk for directions to the "Yellow Point Annex." This is the "Crow and Gate," an authentic English pub about ten miles back toward Cedar. Drink ale and sing, throw darts, and have good British food, too—if you can eat more after Yellow Point's frequent meals.

Dining

Like everything at Yellow Point, dining is a unique experience. There is so much eating to be done that one has to make an effort to work it all in! Besides three hearty regular meals, coffee is served at midmorning before the fireplace in the main room, and tea is served there in the late afternoon and again as a bedtime snack, often with a glass of sherry.

The day begins between eight-thirty and nine-thirty with a farm breakfast in the big dining room. All the guests are seated together at long tables, where everyone quickly gets to know everyone else. Breakfast is an example of home cooking at its best, as is the typical lunch of soup, salad, a soufflé or some other hot dish, fruit, and dessert.

Dinner is at half-past six, when the gong is rung to alert guests. Often during the summer the meal is served outdoors at the big barbecue

Luncheon on the lawn at Yellow Point Lodge

pit, where salmon or steelhead are grilled, perhaps along with one's own catch of delicacies. Otherwise, dinner is served in the dining room in the same community style as the other meals.

Although wine and beer are available with meals, they are the only items not included on the American plan. Guests can order what they want, however, and the cost is added, with no markup, to their bill. Yellow Point, by the way, presents only one bill, on the day of departure. Any gratuities to the staff are left at the same time, deposited in a big glass jar on the front desk.

Bedwell Harbour Resort

Distances:

From Seattle—148 miles, plus ferry; allow 6 hours

From Portland—323 miles, plus ferry; allow 9 hours

From Vancouver, B.C.—25 miles, plus ferry; allow 4 hours

Features:

Brand new resort, completely rebuilt in 1980, on a picturesque harbor in the Gulf Islands; includes a pub, restaurant, store, marina with complete boaters' facilities, plus attractive shore accommodations; secluded ocean beaches and beautiful sunsets

Activities:

Boat watching, sunbathing, swimming, bicycling, picnicking

Seasons:

15 April through 1 October, when the restaurant is in operation, is the main season; the pub, with limited food service, and the living units are open year-round

Rates:

$42 (Canadian currency) for two people in a hotel unit; $45 for two people in a cabin; $54 to $62 for four people in a cabin

Address:

South Pender Island, B.C. V0N 2T0, Canada

Phone:

(604) 629-3488

Bedwell Harbour Inn resembles Old English village

Long ago Bedwell Harbour was dubbed "God's Pocket" by mariners who looked forward to its snug, sheltered moorage, as well as the tranquil beauty of the setting. Then as now, it was further appreciated for its easy accessibility, being centrally located on South Pender Island in the San Juan—Gulf Island chain. Hedged in by great rock cliffs, the resort is compactly arranged at the head of the harbor's innermost cove.

Long and fondly known to the boating fraternity, the original rustic inn that occupied the site burned down one Halloween eve several years ago. The inn was completely redesigned and rebuilt by a new owner in time for the 1980 season, and returning old-timers will be surprised by the imposing complex of glistening white buildings capped by steep, dark roofs that now greets them.

A long dock with tie-up facilities for sixty boats extends directly out from the resort. During the season it can be counted on to fill up with a colorful array of boats from all around the Northwest. Frequently there is an overflow with latecomers dropping anchor outside the log boom to row in by dinghy. Some of the boats come for a single night, others tie up for days. Their passengers use the showers provided by the resort, eat lunch in the courtyard outside the snack bar, swim in the pool, buy supplies at the store, and have dinner at the restaurant. Sixty boats mean about 250 people, which adds up to a colorful, friendly crowd.

Resident guests of the resort itself make up a minority of the people, but they fit in easily and enjoy the special atmosphere imported by the mariners. From their balconies or the veranda of the pub they can oversee the activity on the dock and the boats in the harbor. And with evening come resplendent sunsets across the harbor, making a spectacular backdrop for the diners at the restaurant's outdoor dining area.

Routes and Distances

Getting to Bedwell Harbour is easy for those with their own boat. It is a short run from the San Juans or any of the cities north of Anacortes, and there is a customs house right at the end of the dock, making it especially convenient for Americans to check in.

Otherwise, you come to the Pender Islands by ferry, either with an automobile or a bicycle (bicycles are rapidly gaining favor because in the busy summer months motor vehicles sometimes must wait in long lines to get aboard and because the fare for bicycles is considerably lower than that for autos). There are lots of ferries and many scheduling intricacies to understand in order to make the best use of them. Refer to the chapter on Pender Lodge for a discussion of this subject. Pender Lodge is close to the Otter Bay ferry terminal on the north island, while Bedwell Harbour is twenty minutes away by auto, on South Pender.

Accommodations

Many more people sleep on their boats than ashore at Bedwell Harbour, but nevertheless there is a brand new two-story hotel unit built into the hillside and five older log cabins that have been completely refurbished and modernized available for those who come by ferry.

When you look toward shore from the end of the long dock, the resort has the appearance of an old English village, with an assortment of buildings constructed of white stucco and dark-colored half-beams and trim. At the water's edge is the pub, which has a balcony furnished with umbrella tables and chairs and is a popular place from which to observe the activities in the harbor.

Behind the pub is a courtyard giving access to the snack bar, grocery store, showers, and teen-agers' game room. On the hill above this group of buildings is the restaurant and the new hotel units and cabins. There are ten units in the new building, all identical except that the ones on the top level have a better view of the harbor. Since they all rent for the same price, you may want to request a top floor room if one is available. Each room has a deck and is spacious and comfortably furnished. The couch is a hide-a-bed, so the quarters can accommodate four, but not without crowding. Small kitchenettes with basic utensils make breakfast or lunch an easy matter.

The five cabins higher on the hill are scattered to afford 180-degree views of the harbor. Though they retain the informality of log structures, they now have big picture windows that make them bright and cheerful. The cabins have fully equipped kitchens with modern fixtures, cozy living areas with metal fireplaces, and modern baths, and four of them have two bedrooms with spacious closets. These make ideal accommodations for two couples. The fifth cabin is called the "honeymoon cottage" and is a studio unit having the same kitchen and living area as the other cabins but all in one large room.

Activities

The favorite activity of everbody, boaters and nonboaters alike, is strolling up and down the docks, inspecting other people's boats and gear and looking for old friends. Life-styles afloat are quite different from those on land, but it is possible to imagine from the kind of rigging and equipment on each boat how people live and cope on shipboard, and this kind of conjecturing is a pleasant occupation that consumes a good deal of everyone's time.

When the sun climbs over the hills in midmorning and hits the swimming pool, the center of activity shifts there. The pool area quickly fills up with sunbathers and swimmers. Behind the pool is a big array of black rubber solar panels, facing south to catch the sun's rays; they heat the

Boats dock in front of Bedwell Harbour Inn

pool to a pleasant temperature and also are a lively topic of conversation about how they work.

After a morning of boat watching and swimming, a picnic lunch is an appealing option, and a good place to have it is out on Indian Point, which is a five-minute walk through the woods east of the cabin area. The point is a strikingly pretty place, still owned by native Indians, who camp there overnight once each year to reestablish their rights to the property. The "point," though, is actually a series of grassy bluffs ranging along the harbor edge with half a dozen tiny, secluded sand and shell beaches between them. You can picnic on the knolls or down on the beaches—both choices are sunny and wind sheltered. There is always a procession of boats to watch, and if a dip in bracing cold water is your kind of swimming, this is a good place for it.

Many people come to Bedwell Harbour by bicycle to avoid waiting in long ferry lines or to save on the ferry fare, but the Penders are also fun to explore by bike. The ride from Otter Bay to the resort is twelve miles, with particularly interesting scenery near the bridge between the two islands. The road is not without hills, but they are the short, rolling kind that most bikers can handle, and the auto traffic is almost always light.

View of the harbor from Indian Point

Dining

In spite of the pleasant appointments inside Bedwell Harbour's newly decorated restaurant, the choice spot to dine on nice summer evenings is the huge deck overlooking the water. Like the deck on the pub below, it is furnished with comfortable cushioned chairs and tables that have colorful umbrellas to protect diners from the glare of the setting sun. Since the harbor is so sheltered, wind is rarely a problem.

Because of the resort's distance from the source of supply in the city, the dinner menu in the restaurant is limited, not only as a matter of expediency but also in the interest of quality. The regular menu contains five standard entrées, such as two different cuts of steak, a seafood dish, and perhaps spareribs and game hen, and each evening there is a specialty of the house. Salad from the well-stocked salad bar and hot whole wheat bread round out the meal. A good choice of wine is available, and it is worth noting that besides domestic house wine, excellent imported French wine is sold by the carafe at only a slightly higher price.

Breakfast is also served seven days a week during the season, but the restaurant is closed at lunchtime. Then guests can use the window service at the snack bar in the courtyard, or whip up something for themselves in their kitchenettes, or, as many do, go to the beach under the bridge or to Indian Point for a picnic.

Pender Lodge

Distances:
>From Seattle—136 miles, plus ferry; allow 5 to 6 hours
>From Portland—311 miles, plus ferry; allow 8½ hours
>From Vancouver, B.C.—13 miles, plus ferry; allow 3 hours

Features:
>Close-in but seemingly remote location on the "prettiest of the Gulf Islands"; area has low rainfall with the mildest climate in Canada; accessible only by ferry—getting there is sometimes complicated but also can be fun

Activities:
>Swimming, tennis, lawn games, boating, fishing; golf nearby

Seasons:
>Year-round, but slack in winter when fewer activities are available

Rates:
>$22 to $35 for two people

Address:
>Pender Island, B.C. V0N 2M0, Canada

Phone:
>(604) 629-3221

Pender Lodge was originally a private mansion

Spring of 1980 found the new owners of Pender Lodge deep in renovations getting ready for the summer season. Pender Lodge is an old place, and maintaining its charm requires a great deal of loving care. It is fortunate that it is receiving this special attention, because for sixty years the lodge has been a haven to Canadians wanting to get away from it all. Its location, so close to the major cities of Victoria and Vancouver, renders this place particularly attractive for the quick getaway and explains why many vacationing families routinely come back here, year after year.

Pender Island has a quiet, sleepy-paced tempo. There is no commerce, and the small permanent population is made up mainly of retirees who prize the serene life. The climate seems to promote longevity, for as one native joked, "If the average life expectancy of men is sixty-nine years and of women seventy-two, the average age on this island is dead!" Conditions seem to be good for life in general. Besides people, deer thrive here, too: the island is loaded with them, and drivers must be careful because the deer are seldom hunted and thus are not wary of man or automobiles.

It is the tourists who keep things humming. They arrive by boat at the marina (where the lodge van will pick them up) or by car or bike on the ferries. Made up mostly of Canadians until recently, the guest register now is being augmented by Americans who want to keep gasoline costs down by vacationing close to home and have discovered that they benefit from the favorable exchange rate when traveling in Canada. The especially reasonable prices charged by this lodge add to those advantages, so a higher proportion of Americans seems to be ensured during the decade of the eighties.

Routes and Distances

Although Pender Island, as one of the Canadian Gulf Islands, seems remote to Americans, it actually is only two miles from the United States border and five miles from the closest of the San Juans. An extensive ferry system operated by the government of British Columbia services these islands with boats originating on the mainland and Vancouver Island. There are also inter-island ferries plying between the major ports in the Gulf chain, so that, all told, at least ten boats per day stop at Pender's Otter Bay terminal, which is only a third of a mile from Pender Lodge.

An astute student of ferry schedules can work out a number of itineraries for getting to Pender, but the quickest way from either Vancouver or Seattle is via the Tsawwassen ferry, whose busy terminal is thirteen miles south of Vancouver. The ferry ride itself takes one hour and forty-five minutes. The most convenient run leaves Tsawwassen every day at mid-morning and arrives at Pender around noon. Reservations can be made for this trip, and they are a must during busy weekends and in summer. Even when you have a reservation, it is necessary to get to the terminal forty-five minutes before the scheduled sailing time, and without reservations, in the busy summer season, step that up one to two hours to be sure of getting aboard. (There are afternoon ferries, too, but the schedules change with the season and the boats leave at different times on different days, with most of them arriving at Pender in the late evening. It is always important to double-check ferry schedules for revisions.)

For Americans, an alternative is to take the Washington State ferry from Anacortes to Sidney on Vancouver Island and then make the five-minute drive to Swartz Bay and transfer to the Canadian ferry to Pender. This route takes a total of seven hours and fifteen minutes, which is longer than the Tsawwassen route, but it may be more convenient and it is scenic and relaxing all the way. (Reservations can be made on this run, two days or more in advance in summer.) The Anacortes ferry leaves at 8:40 A.M., arriving at Sidney at noon. There is plenty of time for lunch at Sidney, as the ferry to Pender does not leave until 3:15. Ask directions to the nearby Latch Restaurant for a rewarding luncheon experience. Arrival time at Pender is 3:55 via this route.

Those with bicycling experience ought to consider leaving their autos at Anacortes or Tsawwassen and bicycling aboard. This eliminates having to wait in line for the ferry, no matter how long the line of cars. Moreover, it costs much less, and no one really needs an auto on Pender Island anyway.

Ferry passing in front of Pender Lodge

Information about the ferries can be obtained by calling the numbers listed in "Information Sources" at the end of the book. Ask for specific information and have them send *current* schedules for the San Juan Islands, the Gulf Islands, and the mainland—Vancouver Island runs. (Also see the Bedwell Harbour chapter for more information.)

Accommodations
People should not come to Pender Lodge looking for slick, modern

hotel accommodations. Built in the 1920s as a private mansion and converted to a lodge in the 1930s, the building is reminiscent of the way things
were a number of years ago. The lodge has nine rooms, three of which
have their own baths; the other six all have washbasins and share three
common baths. The rooms are clean and bright and are maintained in the
tradition of the best old-time inns. Every room is different and has a different outlook. Besides the lodge rooms, there are five more accommodations in small cabins clustered nearby. They are ideal for families, and each
cabin has the advantage of a private bath. Two of them have fireplaces. In
every case, prices are modest indeed, making Pender Lodge one of the
Northwest's most economical getaways.

Activities

To see what is going on at Pender Lodge, it is necessary only to look
out the ivy-bordered casements on the view side. Below, on the bluff
overlooking Otter Bay, are a lawn with a tennis court and swiming pool,
and beyond these are the blue channel and its teeming boat traffic as far as
the eye can see.

The court is an old-style pounded clay surface with nailed down tapes,
but it is the only court on the island and the site of lots of happy tennis
matches. The pool is deep enough for diving and relies on the sun for heat,
so swims are brisk and usually are followed by long sunning periods on the
warm concrete deck.

Tennis court and pool at Pender Lodge overlooking strait

Outdoor shuffleboard, horseshoes, and a giant checkerboard also are available on the lawn. Farther afield but less than a mile away is the Pender Island Golf and Country Club. Amazingly, this rolling, beautifully kept little nine-hole course is entirely maintained by volunteers from the community. The green fees are low and paid on the honor system; golfers just put their money through a slot in the wall of the tiny clubhouse. The rules and information are posted, but there are no carts or rentals, so golfers must bring their own equipment.

Bicycling is popular on the island because there is little automobile traffic and drivers are courteous. Island roads are narrow and hilly, but the beauty all around and the many scenic outlooks bicyclists enjoy are adequate compensation for a few sore muscles.

The light traffic also is conducive to walking on the roads. The lane in front of the lodge, for instance, ends a half mile to the north, where a rickety stairway leads down to an isolated beach. Another favorite short hike commences across the road behind the lodge and leads up to "The Summit," a high point with a spectacular view over a wide portion of the Gulf Islands. There is a bench at the top that affords a pleasant chance to sit in the late evening and watch one of the memorable sunsets these islands are so noted for.

The island's marina is in a sheltered cove a quarter mile from the ferry dock in the opposite direction from the lodge. Boats are available there for fishermen (a small store sells tackle and supplies), and there is a group of outdoor tables for picnic lunches.

Dining

The dining room, in a separate building fifty yards from the lodge, serves three meals a day to guests and also is patronized by island residents. The building is utilitarian on the outside but attractive on the inside, and it has a wonderful view of the busy ferry traffic on Swanson Channel, the sunsets to the west, and the dozens of islands in the distance.

Because the lodge is remote from the source of supplies in the city, the menu is purposely short, but it is nevertheless adequate, with steaks, roasts, seafood, and a nightly "special," which is often the best selection. The owners' personal supervision of all phases of food preparation and services ensures good quality and the comfort of guests.

As is common in British Columbia, wines served with meals are either Canadian brands or European. Local tax laws discourage the sale of California wines, but this should be viewed by Americans as an opportunity to make some new discoveries.

If the restaurant is full, guests can wait below in the "holding room," outfitted like an English pub, where drinks are served and live entertainment is provided whenever the owners can persuade a performer to come over to the island.

Jolly Roger Inn

Distances:
From Seattle—185 miles, plus ferry; allow 6½ hours
From Portland—360 miles, plus ferry; allow 10 hours
From Vancouver, B.C.—40 miles, plus ferry; allow 2½ hours

Features:
Modern condominium living on the Sunshine Coast, site of some of the world's finest salmon fishing; complete restaurant and bar facilities; marina

Activities:
Salmon charters year-round, swimming, golf, sight-seeing

Seasons:
Year-round

Rates:
$60 (Canadian currency) plus tax for one bedroom; $65 to $75 plus tax for two bedrooms

Address:
Secret Cove, Rural Route 1, Halfmoon Bay, B.C. V0N 1Y0, Canada

Phone:
(604) 885-5888; in Vancouver, B.C., 684-3541

Condominium units at Jolly Roger Inn overlook Secret Cove

Your first, most gripping impression at the Jolly Roger Inn will be of the panoramic view from your own balcony looking out over Secret Cove, the little island that guards its entrance, the boats parading in and out, the strait, and the blue mountains rising from Vancouver Island beyond.

In 1976 the old Jolly Roger Hotel burned to the ground in a fire that wiped out a favorite headquarters for salmon fishermen. Now a condominium complex has been built in its place, with the units maintained in a rental pool so that the fishermen, plus many other vacationers, have a headquarters again from which to range over British Columbia's famous Sunshine Coast vacationland.

The site is a steep, heavily timbered hillside running down to the narrow, rockbound cove. Jolly Roger's buildings are staggered on the hill and look over the marina at the bottom and the restaurant conveniently located between them and the marina.

Secret Cove is well known as a snug harbor and convenient stopping place for yachtsmen cruising north to places such as Pender Harbour and Desolation Sound. The moorage rates are kept low for guests of the inn, so among the clientele there are always sailors who come in off the strait for a good dinner and a comfortable night ashore. The other guests are condominium owners, those here for the charter boat fishing, and vacationers who are just fond of the Sunshine Coast.

Routes and Distances

The Sunshine Coast is a seventy-mile stretch along the mainland that faces on the Strait of Georgia and runs approximately from Langdale to Lund. B.C. 101 follows its length, but the only access onto the highway for motor vehicles is by ferry either from Horseshoe Bay, north of the city of Vancouver, or from Comox on Vancouver Island. So the story of how to get to the Jolly Roger Inn is the story of the ferry boats. You plan your trip according to the ferry schedule—which varies according to the day of the week and the season—and strive to arrive at the ferry dock sufficiently ahead of time not to miss the boat. Fortunately, there are lots of boats; they leave Horseshoe Bay for Langdale almost hourly all day long for the forty-five-minute crossing. Be sure to get in the Langdale line and not in the Nanaimo line by mistake. If you are too far back to see the directional signs, ask someone ahead of you; the regulars know exactly where to go.

After crossing to Langdale, just follow 101 north for thirty-one miles through Sechelt to Secret Cove. If you are a golfer, note the location of the golf course on the south side of Sechelt as you pass, and if supplies of any kind are needed, Sechelt is the last place to pick them up. Approximately fifteen minutes out of Sechelt there will be signs indicating that you are approaching Halfmoon Bay; Secret Cove is part of this bay. Five minutes after seeing the Halfmoon Bay signs, look for the Jolly Roger's sign on the left.

To come over from Vancouver Island may be more convenient for some; however, this route involves catching two ferries. The M.V. *Sechelt Queen* leaves Comox four times a day for a 1¾-hour crossing to Powell River. Then twenty-one miles south of Powell River take the Saltery River— Earl Cove ferry across the Jervis Inlet. Secret Cove is a twenty-five-minute drive south from Earl Cove on Highway 101.

If you don't want to drive, you can take one of two daily buses that run between Vancouver and Powell River and stop at Secret Cove. The SMT Line's buses leave from the Pacific Stage Lines terminal at 140 Dunsmuir Street. The trip takes approximately three hours. Call (604) 253-8434 for current schedule information.

Accommodations

Construction of the new Jolly Roger was completed just in time for the summer season of 1980, and it therefore still has the advantages and disadvantages of new construction. On the plus side, everything is bright, modern, and immaculate; the only minus is that the landscaping on the steep hillside is immature, creating a slightly bare appearance.

The four separate buildings containing the thirty condominium units are scattered to ensure privacy and maximize views. The buildings are examples of modern Northwest architecture, with steep shingled roofs and natural cedar exteriors. Twenty-four units have two bedrooms, and six have only one. All thirty are spacious and comfortably furnished and have kitchens complete with all utilities, dishwashers, cooking utensils, and tableware. The living areas have sliding glass doors out to the view deck, wood-burning fireplaces, hide-a-bed couches, dinette sets, televisions, and telephones. The bedrooms are furnished with queen-size beds, and the adjoining bathrooms are modern and convenient. All of the one-bedroom units are priced the same, but prices for the two-bedroom apartments, which are identical in floor plan, vary slightly according to the expansiveness of their views.

Activities

Everyone on this part of the coast knows Don MacDonald, the grizzled owner and operator of Jolly Roger's Marina. If you want to charter a boat for salmon fishing, Don is the one to call [the marina's number is (604) 885-3529]. He is in touch with a dozen charter skippers who know the surrounding waters and where and how to fish them. In this particular area, at the bottom of Malaspina Strait, the water is protected by islands that funnel fish into a narrow passage as they migrate south from their northern feeding grounds. From May through mid-October, it is one of the best coho areas to be found anywhere. Beginning in November and on through the winter months, the "springs" (king salmon to Americans) are running. Charter boats out of the marina charge about thirty-five to forty

Fishermen clean their catch on Jolly Roger's dock

Happy fishermen return to Jolly Roger's marina

dollars per hour, including all necessary tackle and bait, for four fishermen, usually for a minimum of four hours.

All swimming at the Jolly Roger is in the resort's own pool; the shore is too steep and rocky for ocean swimming. Although there are beautiful sandy beaches in Buccaneer Bay, across the strait on Merry Island, the only way to get there is by boat, and though it is but a short run, no small boats are available for rent at this writing. (The marina plans to have some kicker boats in a year or so, after some alterations are made to the facilities.)

Local golfers play at the Sunshine Coast Golf and Country Club, a respected nine-hole course twenty minutes back down Highway 101 at Sechelt. For those who feel compelled to play tennis, there are two public walk-on courts in Sechelt, but they are of only medium quality. The other popular activities are exploring the Sunshine Coast or simply relaxing on the Jolly Roger's comfortable balconies to take in the sun and watch the weather change and the sunsets build in the west.

Dining

As with the condominiums, the dining room and lounge area are brand new, but judging from a few sample meals, the management knows what it's doing.

Considering the dining room's outstanding view over the water, with the activity of the marina in the foreground, the nautical theme of the decor is exactly what one would expect. Lots of polished brass, wood, and rope are featured, with an arrangement of flags and fishnetting above the beams in the open ceiling. Small brass lanterns at each table provide dim lighting during the dinner hour, enhancing the view.

The food is not only good but also moderately priced, with a nice variety of seafood and meat entrées, including, for example, poached oysters on a bed of herbed rice, or racks of tender spring lamb with mint sauce. A nice feature of the restaurant is the standing offer to cook the fish you catch, which, in this "hot" fishing area, is indeed no idle proposition!

The dining room is open for service seven days a week for three meals a day, and the Smugglers Lounge next to it opens at nine in the morning and also serves meals for those who want a cozier atmosphere than the dining room offers.

Shawnigan Lake Inn

Distances:
> From Seattle—170 miles, plus ferry; allow 5½ hours
> From Portland—263 miles, plus ferry (via Port Angeles); allow 8 hours
> From Vancouver, B.C.—52 miles, plus ferry; allow 3¼ hours

Features:
> Venerable resort of the old style, with new ideas; a completely equipped facility located on the shore of a pretty lake

Activities:
> Sailing, canoeing, lake swimming, water-skiing, golf, tennis, sun-bathing, lawn games, whirlpool spa, exercise room

Seasons:
> Year-round; summers are heavily booked

Rates:
> $32 to $42 for two people for room only; $68 to $80 for room and meals in summer; $5 less for all rooms from 1 October through 24 May

Address:
> P.O. Box 40, Shawnigan Lake, B.C. V0R 2W0, Canada

Phone:
> (604) 743-2312

Sailboats tied at pier in front of Shawnigan Lake Inn

Situated close to both Victoria and Vancouver, Shawnigan Lake Inn has been a favorite of Canadians since the early 1900s. Burned down and rebuilt, and occasionally added to over the years, it is now a big, white, rambling hotel set among well-kept lawns, with a host of recreational facilities clustered nearby.

A new chapter in the old resort's history began in 1980. Experienced new owners gave the place a different name and started on a sweeping plan of innovation. Their aim was to hold with the old traditions that made the inn famous but at the same time complete a long list of improvements and additions that would add to the guests' comfort and enjoyment.

The first-time visitor to Shawnigan—viewing the expanse of lawn and the waterfront with its dock, sailboats, and swimming raft—is apt to be smitten with delightful indecision: whether to start lazily with a beverage under the umbrellas on the deck, or sunbathe on the lawn, or go for a sail, or try a game of tennis or golf. Everything is close enough to be visible from the room windows and, except for a few specialities such as speedboats and motorized jet skis, is available for guests to use as part of their room tariff.

Routes and Distances

As with the other Vancouver Island resorts, getting to the Shawnigan Lake Inn from any of the mainland cities is a matter of understanding ferry schedules. It is always advisable to call the ferry terminal in advance to confirm sailing times, which change from season to season, and to ascertain how long a waiting time they anticipate for any particular run.

The inn itself is on the upper end of Shawnigan Lake, forty-five minutes north of Victoria. From Vancouver, take either the Nanaimo ferry from Horseshoe Bay or the Swartz Bay ferry from Tsawwassen. Boats run almost hourly on both of these routes and take one hour and forty-five minutes to make the trip. The fares are identical: sixteen dollars for an auto with two passengers. From Nanaimo to the inn is a forty-two mile drive. From Swartz Bay the trip around Saanich Inlet and up to Shawnigan Lake is approximately fifty miles.

Americans can take the Washington State ferry from Anacortes to Sidney or drive north across the border to catch the Tsawwassen ferry. The total time to the destination is about the same, but the Anacortes ferry makes only one run per day, leaving at 8:40 A.M. It is a scenic ride, however, passing through the heart of the San Juan Islands, touching at Lopez, Shaw, Orcas, and Friday Harbor before proceeding to Sidney where it docks at exactly noon. The cost is twenty-six dollars for an auto

Patio and cabins at Shawnigan Lake

and two passengers. (Sidney and Swartz Bay are just five minutes apart at the tip of the Saanich Peninsula, thirty-one miles from Victoria.)

From Portland use the Seattle routes or, more directly, drive 245 miles to Port Angeles and take the Black Ball ferry *Coho* to Victoria. It leaves four times per day in summer, two or three in other seasons, for a 1½-hour crossing of the Strait of Juan de Fuca. Like the Anacortes ferry, the cost is twenty-six dollars for an auto and two passengers. Call (206) 622-2222 for information.

Accommodations

The modernization program is making sweeping changes at Shawnigan Lake. A number of lovely deluxe units, including some suites with their own private outside entrances, have been created in both wings of the main building. All of the other rooms have been freshly painted, recarpeted, and furnished with new queen-size beds and Tudor-period furniture.

Except for the new suites and a few rooms located in small separate buildings on the lawn, Shawnigan Lake Inn is still basically a resort hotel, and the guest rooms are typical hotel rooms, opening onto long halls on its several floors. The rooms differ in size and shape, partly because the buildings were built and added to at various times. Common to the standards of fifty years ago, some do not have private bathrooms, but share baths across the hall instead (and have correspondingly lower rates). All the rooms are clean and neat, and some are quite spacious; many have good views across the grounds and lake.

Activities

At Shawnigan the main focus of activity is along the 500 feet of level waterfront. From the lakeside rooms, one can look across the broad lawn and see several varieties of sailboats bobbing along the pier leading out to the boathouse. All of these boats are available to guests who have the skills to maneuver them, and for those who don't, the competent staff offers sailing lessons. Besides a fleet of sporty little twelve-foot Lazers, there are some larger varieties available. Guests are also invited to use the hotel's waterbikes, rowboats, and canoes to paddle around the beautiful lake and enjoy the sights.

The newest attractions on the lake are high-powered jet-ski boats that propel a single passenger, sitting or standing, at an exciting thirty-five miles per hour. Conventional water-ski rigs are also available, as well as instruction in the techniques. Finally, for those traveling to the resort with their own boats, the hotel provides an easy-access launching ramp.

Groups of lawn furniture are scattered over the broad expanse of grass, a perfect vantage point to watch all the action. Besides the boating activity, the roped-off swimming area, with its high diving tower and ex-

Boathouse and dock at Shawnigan Lake

ceptionally long slide into the water, is a favorite of all ages. In good weather, the lawn itself becomes a playground for volleyball, badminton, shuffleboard, and horseshoes.

On the other side of the inn, there are two high-fenced asphalt tennis courts, lighted for night play, and, just up the hill, a little par-three nine-hole golf course. For more challenging golf, the fine Cowichan Golf Club is nearby, and soon the indoor swimming pool, Jacuzzi, sauna, and racquetball court will be ready for action.

Dining

The first phase of the new owners' renovation program was to rebuild completely the whole front desk and lobby and the food service areas. The latter are now known as the Hideaway Restaurant and the Retreat Lounge. Both were designed with wide windows looking out over the dockside activity and with easy access onto a deck furnished with lots of brightly colored umbrellas. Both rooms have high beamed ceilings and individually dim-lit tables, with the dining part broken up by a system of paned-glass dividers into small, intimate areas. The decoration scheme features blowups of photographs of the resort the way it appeared in its early years. The focal point of the whole area is a big stone fireplace with a traditional ship model on the mantel.

The Hideaway is a first-class restaurant that serves three meals a day, with complete menus and moderate prices. Food service is also available in the lounge, which often features live entertainment and dancing in the evening.

Above the restaurant is another bar and lounge room that opens to a much larger deck than the restaurant's, with more tables and beach umbrellas. This area is frequently used for parties and also for light meals and beverages during the day. Its particularly fine view makes it a favorite place for guests to gather.

The Village Green at Vernon

Distances:

From Seattle—393 miles; allow 8 hours

From Portland—545 miles; allow 12 hours

From Vancouver, B.C.—317 miles; allow 6½ hours

Features:

Luxurious resort hotel with complete facilities, deep in the Okanagan country where sunshine and dry air prevail

Activities:

Alpine skiing nearby, tennis, swimming, Jacuzzi, nightclub

Seasons:

Year-round

Rates:

$44 for two people in a standard room, $47 with kitchenette; during ski season children under eight are free, other seasons children under fourteen are free; economical six-day winter ski packages available

Address:

Highway 97 and Silver Star Road, Vernon, B.C. V1T 4Z1, Canada

Phone:

(604) 542-3321; collect calls accepted from all parts of the Northwest

Rooms at Village Green overlook enclosed courtyard

Tucked in between the headlands of two beautiful lakes, Kalamalka Lake and Lake Okanagan, the town of Vernon makes an ideal starting point for exploring the sunny cattle country, hunting in the fall, skiing the mountains in the winter, and fishing all year-round.

The Village Green Inn is not only a good headquarters for all these activities, but it is also a self-contained vacation complex that provides, right on the premises, just about everything required for a good time. Thus, you can fly in and spend a few days without even needing an automobile. In fact, so many guests arrive by air that during the ski season the inn provides a daily shuttle-bus service to the mountain.

Upon first arriving at the Village Green you may be disappointed that it is not in the fanciest part of town but is situated in a row of commercial buildings across from a shopping center. Once inside, however, all that becomes irrelevant. What sets this resort apart from others is the quality and completeness of all of its services and appointments. As if one swimming pool were not enough, it has two. As if outdoor tennis were not enough, it has both indoor and outdoor. As if one restaurant were not enough, it has two, plus two lounges, and food and drink service on the patio. The rooms and lobby are luxuriously furnished, the gardens well tended, and the gift shop and newsstand well stocked. It is, in short, an unexpected discovery in an unexpected location.

Routes and Distances

From Vancouver take the Trans-Canada Highway through Cache Creek and Kamloops to Monte Creek, where B.C. 97 branches off to the right. Follow 97 sixty-two miles to Vernon. The alternate way is to leave the Trans-Canada Highway at Hope and follow B.C. 3 to Keremeos and 3A from there to the intersection with 97, just below Penticton. Vernon is seventy miles north of Penticton. You will find the Village Green Inn on the north side of town at the intersection of 97 and Silver Star Road.

From Seattle the shortest way is Washington 20 to Omak, then north on 97 to Vernon. When the North Cascades passes are closed by snow in winter, cross either Stevens or Snoqualmie Pass, join U.S. 97, and follow it north.

From Portland drive east on Interstate 84 to Biggs and then follow 97 all the way to Vernon.

The airline that serves the Vernon-Kelowna area is Pacific Western, which has five to seven flights per day from Vancouver. Call (604) 684-6161 in Vancouver and (206) 433-5088 in Seattle for reservations and information, and advise the inn of your flight schedule in advance. They will provide transportation from the airport, about a forty-minute drive from the resort.

Patio and pool overlook tennis court at Village Green

Patio area of Village Green

Accommodations

The Spanish architecture of the inn is reflected in the interior as well as the facade of the building. Wide hallways are paved with polished brick and offer occasional glimpses through the windows into small, intimate interior courtyards containing fountains surrounded by pretty shrubbery.

The two types of accommodations most suitable for couples are similar in floor plan, with just one basic variation: one has a kitchenette, the other does not. Though compact, the kitchenette is convenient and fully equipped with dishes and cooking utensils. In every other respect the rooms are the same, with a bath, a dressing area, a patio or deck, double or twin beds, a sofa, and a small game table with chairs.

For those who desire additional roominess, however, there are larger quarters available. Besides some suites, there are a number of bedroom—sitting room combinations, at correspondingly higher prices, of course.

Activities

The Village Green can match any resort of its type for summer activities, and few resorts can match its unique winter program.

For summer fun the inn has a large outdoor area bordered on three sides by the rambling structure of the hotel. Within this area are a swimming pool, a Jacuzzi, a sunken championship tennis court, and umbrella tables and chairs from which to watch the activity. On the edge of the compound is a fully equipped tennis pro shop where all reservations are handled. On the other side of the pro shop are four more tennis courts. When winter comes and the weather turns cold a bubble is put over this group of courts, and the tennis activity goes on year-round.

But the big thing in winter is skiing. The Village Green is just thirteen miles from the fine Silver Star ski area, which has eight lifts—three of them chair lifts—serving runs for skiers of every ability. One of the chair lifts is over a mile long with a 1,600-foot vertical drop. A fully equipped ski shop, as well as a large day lodge and restaurant and lounge, is located at the summit.

Having a first-rate ski area so close to luxury accommodations in itself is appealing, but the bonus here is that skiers can return from the slopes to play a game of tennis, swim in the indoor pool, or take a sauna, then enjoy fine dining and a swinging nightclub—all right on the premises.

To make all of this as attractive as possible, each winter the inn offers ski packages that usually include the room, taxes, and lift tickets. For example, in 1981 a six-day package for a couple costs $352, with meals and incidentals not included. These packages change from time to time, however, so it is advisable to call the reservations desk for information about the current plan.

Dining

Hy's Steak House, adjoining the Village Green lobby, is known throughout British Columbia for its fine cuisine. Open only for dinner, it has a plush atmosphere and a tempting selection of meats, seafood, and fine wine.

For a less formal evening, the Coffee Garden, also just off the lobby, serves good food and is a pleasant place for dinner. It is also open for breakfast and lunch.

In good weather, you may have the most fun lunching outdoors at the umbrella tables off the Patio Lounge. From here, you can watch the activity in the pool and on the sunken tennis court. The food is served buffet style from eleven-thirty to two, and it is sumptuous—you can take as much as you like of whatever you want. Sports attire, including swimming outfits, is acceptable at this informal and friendly gathering place.

Campbell's Lodge

Distances:
>   From Seattle—185 miles; allow 3½ hours
>   From Portland—329 miles; allow 6½ hours
>   From Vancouver, B.C.—266 miles; allow 5 hours

Features:
>   Big, long established, and well-known resort on the warm southern tip of Lake Chelan, where sunshine, dry air, and clear water prevail

Activities:
>   Sailing, water-skiing, fishing, swimming, water volleyball, sunbathing, hot spa; golf and tennis nearby; boat trips into the heart of the Cascades; browsing in shops and galleries

Seasons:
>   Rooms available year-round, but the restaurant and cottages close for the off-season, 1 November through 1 April

Rates:
> $52 to $64 per day for two people in summer; lower off-season rates; $378 to $630 per week for four to six people in a housekeeping cottage

Address:
>   P.O. Box 278, Chelan, Washington 98816, U.S.A.

Phone:
>   (509) 682-2561

Historic Campbell House Restaurant

Campbell's Lodge is like Topsy—it just grew, and it has continued to grow and change for the last eighty years. It all began when Clinton Cyrus Campbell, the first of four generations of owners, came out from Sioux City, Iowa, and, taken with the land around the beautiful blue waters of Lake Chelan, proceeded to buy a piece that included half of the present town for $400. When the sale was consummated, the seller told the boys at the local tavern he had "just sold a sandlot to a sucker." But it was Mr. Campbell who had the last laugh.

In those early days there was a military outpost at Chelan to protect settlers from the Indians, and many travelers from the east passed through by stage. Clint Campbell, thinking a hostelry to provide lodging and good food was in order, built the Hotel Chelan on his new property. Later the hotel became known as the Campbell House, and today the same building is still the focal point of the large resort complex that has grown around it.

Early in the 1940s several groups of housekeeping cottages went up, and these are still very much in demand. The first modern two-story hotel unit was constructed in the 1950s, followed by a second one a decade later, and a third in the 1970s. Much of the original land was sold along the line or taken through the laws of eminent domain, which allow the government to take land for necessary public use. So the growth phase is finally over. No room is left for more buildings, but a first-class resort, the name of which many think is synonymous with a Lake Chelan vacation, remains to honor the original Mr. Campbell.

Routes and Distances

From Seattle drive across Snoqualmie Pass to Cle Elum and from there take Washington 970 to U.S. 97. Highway 97 crosses Swauk Pass, a scenic drive at any time of year, and comes down into the beautiful orchard country surrounding Peshastin and Cashmere. Continue on 97, which soon begins to follow the Columbia River north, past Rocky Reach Dam and through a wide, spectacular stretch of river valley. Just to see this bit of Eastern Washington almost in itself makes the trip worthwhile. Arriving in Chelan, you can find Campbell's Lodge on the west side of town, right on the lake.

The shortest way from Vancouver is over the North Cascades Highway, Washington 20, from Burlington to Twisp, then south on Washington 153 to Pateros. At Pateros pick up U.S. 97 and continue south for twenty more miles to Chelan.

From Portland take Interstate 84 east to Biggs, cross the Columbia on U.S. 97, and remain on 97 through Yakima and Ellensburg, over Swauk Pass, and all the way to Chelan.

Following the Columbia en route to Lake Chelan

Lake and beach as seen from Campbell's Lodge room

Accommodations

In the diverse accommodations at Campbell's Lodge, there are 100 separate units with a total capacity of over 300 people. Three modern two-story buildings have 83 units that are rented year-round. They vary in size from a bedroom with a double bed, a dressing alcove, a bath, and a deck overlooking the lake to suites that accommodate up to six persons. Higher summer rates for these units are in effect from the middle of June through Labor Day. The other units consist of seventeen fully furnished house-keeping cottages, which are scattered around the property and are rented during only the summer months on a weekly basis. The cottages right on the beach are slightly more expensive than those set back on the property. All of the cottages accommodate four to six people, and daily maid service is provided.

Activities

The city of Chelan has a permanent population of three thousand, which swells to five times that many in the summer, because visitors are its principal industry. To augment the natural enticements of blue sky, dry air, sun, and beautiful, clear water, nearly everything else that might attract vacationers has also been made available somewhere in the area. And Campbell's Lodge is located strategically so its guests can participate in all the activities.

The lodge's property has white sand beaches directly in front of the buildings, and the sandy lake-bottom slopes gently from the shore, making ideal conditions for wading and swimming. There are boat docks (boaters can bring in their own boats and use a public launching ramp at nearby Lakeshore Park to put them in the water), a separate swimming dock with a diving board, rafts and inner tubes, a net in the shallows for water volleyball, and barbecue pits at the water's edge. Water-skiers, sailboats, fishermen, and mariners who are "just cruising" crisscross the lake, while sun-seekers lounge on the beach and grass. The water in Lake Chelan is icy cold in the deep northern stretches, but it is shallow at this end and is a pleasant temperature by early summer. If it is not just right, however, you can swim in the big pool on the front lawn or the smaller one, which has glass windscreens, behind the restaurant. A hot spa, big enough for a dozen people, is sunk in the lawn next to the larger pool.

No tennis courts are available on lodge property, but there are two municipal courts at Lakeshore Park and four more at the high school, three blocks from the lodge. Golfers can play an eighteen-hole public course, fully equipped with a clubhouse and teaching pros, located a mile and a half from the resort on a plateau looking down on the lake and valley. The lake is well known for its game fish, and smaller lakes and streams in the vicinity yield trout and steelhead. In town there are craft shops and galleries, a museum that specializes in the early history of the area, and a summer theater that offers performances nightly, Tuesday through Sunday.

Finally, most of those who visit Chelan devote one day to taking the excursion vessel, *Lady of the Lake,* into the Cascade wilderness at the fjordlike head of the lake. Every day in summer and four times a week in winter she leaves Chelan at half-past eight in the morning for the fifty-five mile voyage to Stehekin. The boat has a snack bar for refreshments en route. A two-hour lunch stop at the North Cascades Lodge allows plenty of time to explore before reboarding for the return trip.

Dining

The Campbell House Restaurant is located on the lower level of the old hotel building, just as it was originally. It is a pleasant setting for the three meals that are served seven days a week during the summer season. The restaurant opens at 6:45 A.M. for the convenience of guests taking the boat trip to Stehekin.

In nice weather, lunch also is served on the second-floor covered veranda, where tables are set with red-checkered tablecloths and planter boxes along the railing are filled with gay summer flowers. Guests can look out over the lake while relaxing in the warm air and sunshine. The menu on the veranda is limited to sandwiches and salads but is quite sufficient.

Campbell House has long been famous for its dinners, not only among guests at the resort but also among visitors from throughout the Chelan area. It offers a full menu with a good wine list. A large, comfortable bar and lounge upstairs are decorated in the old style and have many nostalgic photographs.

For dining variety, the best alternate place in the vicinity is the Ellowee Beach Restaurant at Wapato Point, five miles up the lake on the south side of Manson. It has a lovely dining room and, for even more fun on summer evenings, a big barbecue deck where informal dinners are served.

North Cascades Lodge

Distances:

From Seattle—185 miles, plus boat or air trip up Lake Chelan; allow at least 1 day .

From Portland—329 miles, plus boat or air trip; allow 1 day

From Vancouver, B.C.—266 miles, plus boat or air trip; allow 1 day

Features:

Remote, rustic resort nestled in the astonishingly beautiful North Cascade Mountains

Activities:

Fishing, hiking, bicycling, photography, and nature watching in summer; snowshoeing, cross-country skiing, and nature watching in winter

Seasons:

Year-round; winter ski packages available

Rates:

$29 to $47 for two people; $44 to $54 in a housekeeping unit

Address:

Stehekin, Washington 98852, U.S.A.

Phone:

The lodge itself can be contacted directly only via radio-telephone from Chelan; an office is maintained in Chelan to arrange reservations: call (509) 682-4711; Chelan Airways, at 682-5555, also maintains radio contact with the lodge.

Entrance to North Cascades Lodge

If ever there were a resort at "the end of the line," the North Cascades Lodge is it, located deep in the Lake Chelan National Recreation Area with not a single road leading in or out.

Part of the fun is getting there by air or via a leisurely cruise on the *Lady of the Lake*. The boat leaves Chelan each morning and takes four hours to make the trip up Lake Chelan's narrow gorge, carved through the mountains by glaciers thousands of years ago. It usually is loaded with day passengers, out for the sight-seeing, with only a sprinkling of people going to the North Cascades Lodge to stay. When the vessel ties up at the Stehekin dock, the hungry crowd swarms up to the lodge restaurant to have lunch on the big deck facing the waterfront. There, tables are arranged under spreading shade trees that grow right through the decking. As the passengers eat and admire the surrounding scenery, frequent remarks are sure to be overheard about the magnificent beauty of the place. But it is not until the round-trippers go back on board and the boat leaves for its return journey that those who remain begin to feel the true seclusion of Stehekin. It is the beginning of a unique experience that will be remembered long after other vacations have been forgotten.

Routes and Distances

There are three ways to get to Stehekin: fly from Chelan via Chelan

Airways, cruise up on the *Lady of the Lake,* or hike in over Cascade Pass from Western Washington—but only the first two are applicable to this book.

The boat leaves daily at half-past eight in the morning from its dock

Lady of the Lake docked at North Cascades Lodge

a mile west of town. (The schedule is reduced to four times per week in winter.) All along the fifty-five mile trip she puts in at settlements and camps to deliver mail or supplies to isolated residents or to let hikers off. The farther up the lake she gets, the more precipitous and fjordlike the country becomes. Binoculars are essential here, as are cameras with telephoto lenses, for spotting wildlife, especially goats, among the rocky crags.

The Chelan Airways flight affords a completely different perspective of the lake and its surroundings. The little float planes, a de Haviland Beaver that seats six and a Cessna that seats four, are a delightfully easy way to travel. The pilot flies at two thousand feet through the mountainous gorge, which rises five thousand to eight thousand feet on either side. Sometimes the wing tips seem almost to brush the hills, enabling you to examine every detail of mountains and shore.

To take full advantage of the sight-seeing opportunities, many people like to go in by boat and out by air or vice versa. The one-way fare for the *Lady of the Lake* is eight dollars and for the plane twenty-five dollars.

One thing to consider is that although the air fare is more expensive, flying to Stehekin enables you to drive to Chelan from most Northwest cities during the day (with an early start) and catch an evening flight into Stehekin. That saves the price of a room in Chelan for one night, which is necessary when you take the boat because it leaves so early in the morning. This also is true on the return trip, since the boat leaves Stehekin at two o'clock in the afternoon and gets back to Chelan about five. You can plan your own trip accordingly. Up-to-date schedule information can be obtained by calling the boat terminal at (509) 682-2224 or Chelan Airways at (509) 682-5555. For directions to Chelan, see the chapter on Campbell's Lodge.

Accommodations

Two basic types of accommodations are available: lodge rooms and housekeeping units. The lodge rooms are in a two-story motellike building and are priced according to size and view. The larger ones are the most comfortable, but all are adequate; each has its own full bath and either twin or double beds. The housekeeping units are completely furnished cabins and A-frames, each with a full kitchen, scattered close to the other buildings. They are particularly popular with skiers, who can subsist in them comfortably in winter whether the dining room is operating or not. Advance reservations, it should be remembered, are essential for all wintertime occupancies.

Activities

Stehekin is the focal point for a network of trails and backcountry camp areas extending through the North Cascades National Park. Any day, you can see backpackers arriving at the lodge and others leaving for extensive hikes across the mountains via Cascade Pass, or along the Pacific Crest Trail, or to remote lakes for fishing and camping. On her way to Stehekin, the *Lady of the Lake* commonly stops briefly at Fish Creek, seventeen miles down the lake, where she noses into the rocky shore and throws out a gangplank for hikers who want to walk the rest of the way—a two- or three-day journey that takes them through some of the most magnificent of Lake Chelan's scenery.

People staying at the lodge take day hikes up these trails to points of interest in summer, and follow the same routes on cross-country skis or snowshoes in winter. Next to the lodge, the Park Service maintains an office so rangers can aid hikers and skiers, providing maps and advice about trail conditions.

People arriving at Stehekin are usually surprised to see trucks and

One-room log schoolhouse at Stehekin

autos at the landing, but the Park Service maintains some twenty miles of roads to connect the major points of interest and trailheads. (The vehicles are brought up from Chelan by barge.) The Park Service also

Rainbow Falls, a short hike from the lodge

runs a shuttle bus up and down the roads providing a convenient way to see the area, including the impressive Rainbow Falls and the only one-room schoolhouse in the state, which are two things visitors should try not to miss.

If hiking is the first priority in this area, fishing on Lake Chelan and in the hundreds of streams and mountain lakes surrounding it is second. The silvers start running in early May, and Chinook, which can weigh up to twelve pounds, are planted regularly in the lake. Trout season starts in the spring when the streams spew water into the lake and wash down food the fish like. They congregate at the outfalls looking for food, and fishermen troll back and forth looking for the fish. Later, when the waters recede, fly-fishing begins in the streams themselves.

Not everyone comes to Stehekin to hike or fish, however. Half the visitors are content to sit on the broad deck in the sun, watching the lake and mountains, and the hikers and fishermen coming and going. If they should want to venture up the roads a little way, however, a few old bicycles are kept in front of the lodge and are available for rent.

From December to March, things change drastically. Most of the roads are closed by snow and the eighty full-time residents and the children attending the schoolhouse depend on skis for transportation. And that is what visitors come for: cross-country skiing. The lodge offers a number of ski packages and members of the Courtney family, who operate backpacking services in summer, provide ski instruction and take groups on unforgettable overnight tours into wilderness cabins in winter.

Indeed, winter in Stehekin is a remarkable experience. Arrangements must be made in advance, however, because transportation in and out is not as regular as in summer, and food service is provided at the lodge only when a certain quota of guests is in residence. The reservations office at Chelan will provide advice and help in making advance plans.

Dining

The restaurant at the lodge has two chief concerns. One is to take care of the *Lady of the Lake's* luncheon crowd, which on a full boat can amount to hundreds of people. The other is to serve the overnight guests of the lodge.

To expedite matters and maximize the time boat passengers have to enjoy themselves while at Stehekin, lunch is served cafeteria style and offers a selection of premade sandwiches, salads, and homemade pies for which the lodge's bakery is famous. Breakfast and dinner are an entirely different affair, tailored exclusively to the more leisurely pace of overnight guests. And considering that all supplies come in by boat or plane, the outstanding quality the lodge has been able to attain is remarkable. Part of the reason is the little bakery, way out here in the middle of

Waterfront deck at North Cascades Lodge

nowhere, and its baker, who puts in twelve hours a day turning out delicacies much in demand at Chelan but even fresher and better at the lodge.

Dinner is served in a rustic dining room where guests can choose from a regular list of à la carte selections or order one of the night's special entrées, which the waitress will describe. "Miner's Stew," served with the bakery's French bread and accompanied with a carafe of Burgundy, is always a good bet for hungry people at night, and in the morning the country breakfast for two will give even the most active hikers enough fuel for a full day on the trail.

Ross Lake Resort

Distances:

> From Seattle—135 miles; allow 3 hours
> From Portland—310 miles; allow 6 hours
> From Vancouver, B.C.—148 miles, allow 3¼ hours

Features:

> Remote fishing camp in a spectacular location, built entirely on floats and inaccessible by auto; no restaurant, no entertainment, no sport facilities—just tremendous peace and quiet

Activities:

> Fishing, exploring the inner Cascades by boat, canoeing, hiking, picnicking

Seasons:

> 20 June through October; short season and limited accommodations make early reservations necessary

Rates:

> $12 to $25 for two people; $9 to $19 per day for boat rental

Address:

> Rockport, Washington 98283, U.S.A.

Phone:

> Radiotelephone Newhalem 7735, ask for Margueritte Dameron, owner/manager

Floating cabins at Ross Lake Resort

As far as its long-time owner knows, Ross Lake Resort is the only resort in the United States that is totally afloat. The cabins, office, marina, and other buildings are all built on log rafts, not only because the shore is too steep for construction, but also because the resort is totally oriented to the water, the level of which changes through the year, sometimes by 100 feet or more. The reason for this is that Ross Lake provides hydroelectric power for Seattle City Light, and during the winter the water level is drawn down drastically to feed the generators. Although no guests are present then, it is a busy time for the staff, who must continually break the ice and keep floating the resort farther out as the lake recedes. In the spring, when the snow melt refills the lake, they must start moving it back again.

Ross Lake was formed many years ago when the first dam was built across the Skagit River. Since then the dam, visible just south of the resort, has been raised in stages, each time making the lake behind it longer and deeper. The dam is now 500 feet tall, but still another addition is contemplated (proving the wisdom of keeping the resort on floats, for otherwise it would surely be flooded out!).

The history of the resort goes back thirty years to just after the last lift of the dam was completed. The original owner, who conceived the idea of a floating fish camp on the lake, gathered together an assortment of cabins and barracks that were built on rafts and left behind by the woodsmen who logged off the timber in the path of the rising water. About a year after this nucleus had been assembled, a former bomber pilot who was running a little seaplane service and his wife flew in to fish for the bountiful rainbow trout they had heard about. They fell in love with the area and within a year had bought the place and begun to develop it into what it is today.

For a long time, the seaplane was the only way to bring in supplies. Everything else, including the guests, had to come up a mountain trail that rose 500 feet to skirt the dam and then down another trail along the lake to the resort, with the guests carrying their gear and supplies on their backs. Now they can make the trip in a series of boat and truck rides, all through an area of majestic and ever-changing scenery.

Recently the floating complex of old cabins and barracks buildings was supplemented by the addition of eight modern cottages, all built on the spot because there was no other way to get them in.

Routes and Distances

From Vancouver, Seattle, or Portland, drive to Burlington, Washington, on Interstate 5 and turn east on Washington 20. Proceed approximately seventy miles, past Newhalem and Gorge Dam, to Diablo Dam. Be sure to look carefully for the Diablo Dam turnoff, which is on the left six miles past Newhalem. A narrow road winds down a hill to the dam and then takes you directly across the top of the dam to the other

Truck takes resort guests to top of Ross Dam

Passenger boat on Diablo Lake

side. After crossing the dam, turn right and follow the edge of the lake toward the Diablo Resort. In about a quarter mile, near a corrugated iron shed, is a large floating dock with signs designating Ross Lake parking. Park and carry your luggage down to the dock. The tugboatlike *Diablo II* picks up passengers at the dock at eight in the morning and again at three in the afternoon and takes them the length of Diablo Lake to the base of Ross Dam for two dollars per person. The half-hour trip is a spectacular ride through an ever-narrowing fjord with nearly vertical walls on either side.

At Ross Dam, the boat puts in at a small float, where everyone scrambles off with their luggage and transfers to the resort's waiting stake-bed truck which has benches to sit on. When all are aboard, the truck labors up a steep, switchbacked gravel road, in low gear all the way, finally achieving the level of the top of the dam. There, at a float on Ross Lake, a speedboat from the resort meets the truck and whisks the passengers across the lake, dropping each party and their luggage directly at the doorstep of the cottage or cabin to which they have been assigned.

Accommodations

All cabins and barracks together can house up to seventy-five people when every bed is counted. The five older units that were left over from the logging camps are furnished in spartan style, with up to six double bunks with bedding, a big wood stove for both cooking and heating, cooking utensils, a refrigerator, and running water, but no towels and no bathroom. Community sanitary facilities are nearby on a separate float; and on shore, reached by a gangplank, are the showers, located in the only shoreside building in the whole complex.

Two of these older units have only two bunks and are extremely economical for a couple. The larger units usually are taken by groups who fish by day and (sometimes) have glorious poker parties around the big stoves long into the night. Substituting poker for bridge, one group that comes each year takes two units, dubbing one the "cookhouse" and keeping a perpetual bridge game going in the other.

On the other side of the office are the modern cottages, each with a large picture window framing snow-capped Colonial Peak, across the lake to the south. These are really little houses, with electric or propane cookstoves, hot water, refrigerators, and wood-burning fireplaces or gas heat. Each has a bath with a shower, a bedroom with bunk beds, and two or three other beds or studio couches in a spacious living room—kitchen combination. All linens are furnished in the cottages, and rents are based on use by a couple, with additional charges for extra persons.

Activities

Ross Lake must be one of the truly unusual resorts in North America. Just to make the trip and become acquainted with the surrounding mountain vastness is activity enough all by itself. Otherwise,

Rugged Cascade peaks surround Ross Lake

Fishermen return to resort at sunset

people come to Ross Lake primarily for the fishing. Groups come especially for the unique camaraderie that can be experienced only in a remote fishing camp.

Ross Lake is a big lake: its twenty-five-mile length extends through the heart of the Cascades all the way to the British Columbia border. Inaccessible except by the Ross Dam route, it is only lightly fished, and native wild trout thrive in its deep, cool waters. "Red"rainbows are the most abundant species, followed by eastern brook, cutthroat and Dolly Varden.

There is no way to get around at Ross Lake, except by boat, so the resort keeps a marina full of canoes and outboards—all in top condition—and the first thing a new guest does is rent a boat, which he uses or keeps tied up in front of his quarters for the duration of his visit. The favorite ways to fish are trolling with a string of flashers ("pop gear") or casting with a single salmon egg near stream outfalls. It is usually not difficult to catch the limit of one- or two-pound rainbows and an occasional big Dolly with either of these techniques, or by alternately using each of them, which is how most fishermen like to do it.

For scenery, you can take your boat up the lake as far as you want to go, cruising close to the shoreline to watch for birds and animals. A particularly nice destination for a picnic lunch is Devil Creek, eight miles up the lake on the west shore. Spot the creek opening by looking for a foot-bridge on the lakeside trail. It is the only bridge along the shore, so it is not hard to find. Go slowly through the deep water of the creek, between ever-narrowing vertical walls. It is a lovely grotto, fully a quarter-mile long to where the white water starts and the creek is barely wide enough to turn the boat around. Another nice place to take lunch is at the head of Ruby Creek four miles west of the resort, which makes a perfect canoe trip. Paddle to where a log jam blocks the river, and find a trail on the left side that follows the creek. Many good picnic sites are available in this area.

One thing to remember when you come to Ross Lake is to bring rain gear and warm clothes for boat trips away from the resort, because the weather can change quickly and drastically in this inner mountain area. A stuff bag containing a rain parka and sweater for each person is easy to carry and easy to keep track of.

Dining

Dining at Ross Lake is what you make it, because you are strictly on your own. Guests must pack in (or catch) whatever food they will need, and the only recourse for forgotten items is a small supply of canned goods the management keeps for emergencies. The kitchens are pleasant to cook in, however, with adequate supplies of utensils and tableware. If you stay in an older unit, you get the opportunity to revive the lost art of working with a wood stove, and a surprising number of people enjoy the challenge. But whether you have an old or new unit, the atmosphere is so pleasant and the experience so unusual that even if there were a fancy restaurant nearby it is unlikely you could soon be lured away from your floating home.

Roche Harbor Resort

Distances:
> From Seattle—85 miles, plus ferry, allow 6 hours; via plane, flight time 1 hour
>
> From Portland—260 miles, plus ferry; allow 9½ hours
>
> From Vancouver, B.C.—102 miles, plus ferry, allow 6½ hours; via plane from Bellingham, flight time 30 minutes

Features:
> Harbor is perfectly protected by barrier islands and known to many as the boating capital of the San Juans; accommodates up to 200 vessels and offers boaters and other visitors all possible shoreside conveniences and amenities, all steeped in the charm of early Northwest history.

Activities:
> Everything related to boats and the water; tennis, swimming, bicycling, sight-seeing, horseback riding, nightly lounge entertainment

Seasons:
> Hotel and boat-support activities operate year-round; after Labor Day restaurant is open on weekends only, and it closes completely from November through March

Rates:
> $32 to $65 for two people in a hotel room; $63 to $72 for four to six people in a cottage; $53 to $90 for two people in a condominium; off-season discounts for hotel rooms and cottages

Address:
> P.O. Box 1, Roche Harbor, Washington 98250, U.S.A.

Phone:
> (206) 378-2155

Hotel de Haro and restaurant from waterfront

Guests come by land, sea, and air to Roche Harbor Resort, a charming complex built on the southern shore of what is often called the most beautiful and best-sheltered harbor in the San Juans. Since Roche is at the upper end of the island group, it is an ideal spot for mariners to stop to replenish supplies at the general store, shower in the public bathhouse, and have dinner at the inn before cruising on or making a return trip. Other boaters come to tie up for days, or even weeks, and live aboard while enjoying the resort facilities ashore. The result, in the summer season, is a fascinating array of yachts and boats ranged along the docks and constantly coming and going, providing a better exhibition than any boat show—with no tickets to buy.

The other guests, who come by air or ferry, have their choice from a group of modern condominiums along the harbor front, or they can steep themselves in history by putting up at the quaint old Hotel de Haro. This building was once a Hudson's Bay Company trading post built of logs and was remodeled around the old framework in about 1860. Today its floors are not all level and the walls not exactly plumb, but its charm and outlook and wealth of mementos, antiques, and artifacts make it a not-soon-to-be-forgotten experience.

Every evening during the summer a colors ceremony takes place at sunset. Guests come to attention along the docks and all around the resort as the flags are lowered. A group of boys files out on the dock to the tune of the "Colonel Bogey" march, an evening gun booms at the exact moment of sundown, then one by one the flags of the Roche Harbor Yacht Club, Washington, Canada, England, and the United States are lowered, each to the appropriate music. The ceremony ends with "Taps." Witnessing this ceremony in its beautiful natural setting never fails to instill pride and exhilaration, and the feeling that all around are sharing the same thrill.

Eventually winter comes and the harbor has only a few boats scattered along its docks, the garden's color is gone, and the old brick walk is wet and slippery, but people still come to stay in the hotel or hole up in one of the condominiums in front of a fireplace. Why do they come and what do they do at this time of year? The young desk manager, contemplating this question, finally gave us a serious look and said, "We just don't ask."

Routes and Distances

The Seattle-Tacoma airport is only an hour and five minutes from Roche Harbor via San Juan Airlines' five daily flights. At the Roche Harbor end, the airstrip is on top of the hill next to the "Company Town" cottages, and it is an easy walk to the hotel for anyone not loaded with too much baggage. This same busy airline also flies to Roche Harbor from Bellingham several times daily, which is a time-saving convenience for Canadians. (See "Information Sources" at the end of the book for flight information telephone numbers.)

Restaurant and docks at Roche Harbor

Otherwise, ferry schedules dominate travel to the resort, but the ferries run at frequent intervals, making six trips per day from the terminal at Anacortes. Actual trip time is one hour and fifty minutes, but it is necessary to allow anywhere from a half hour to two hours extra, depending on the season, to get in line and ensure a place on the desired boat. A check with the ferry company in advance is always advisable.

The ferry docks on San Juan Island at the picturesque village of Friday Harbor, a ten-mile drive from Roche Harbor. Because the ride between the two places is easy and scenic, an increasing number of people leave their autos at the Anacortes parking lot and wheel their bicycles aboard the ferry. Bikes are first on and first off, so there is no waiting in line, and of course they enjoy much lower fares than automobiles. If the weather projection sounds favorable, this is a travel option to consider.

The Anacortes terminal is actually five miles west of the town. Take Interstate 5 to Burlington, then turn west on Route 20 and follow the signs through Anacortes.

Accommodations

Hotel de Haro is still the favorite spot for many guests, in spite of the modern facilities added in recent years. The venerable building, with its second story veranda and tangled growth of ivy on the facade, stands right in the heart of the activity like a proud Victorian lady.

The hotel has twenty rooms, and since it was built at a time when indoor plumbing was a luxury, it is surprising that there are even four suites with private baths. One other room has a half-bath, and the rest have basins, with communal baths down the hall. The rooms are nevertheless clean and comfortable, all furnished with antiques and wallpapered with patterns from another era.

The spanking new condominiums are a different world, just a five-minute walk around the harbor to the west. As in most condominium developments, these are all privately owned and when their owners are not using them are maintained in a rental pool available to the general public. The smallest units are typical studios, consisting of a large bedroom with a fireplace, balcony, and bath. The next smallest have a big living room with a fireplace, hide-a-bed sofa, kitchen, and dining alcove, and a balcony and bath. After that are a variety of one-, two-, and three-bedroom units that can accommodate up to eleven people.

A third type of accommodations is the "Company Town Cottages" near the airstrip. Originally built by the lime company for its supervisors, these houses have been remodeled for family use and are rented by the week during the peak season.

Activities

A great deal of strolling takes place here: past the ancient lime kilns

Bicyclist stops to enjoy harbor scene

built when Great Britain and the United States jointly occupied the island; along the harbor-front road to Afterglow Point; among the gardens and along the promenade in front of the hotel; up the hill to the mausoleum; and along the network of docks to inspect boats and greet boaters.

Literally and figuratively, Roche Harbor is a colorful place to explore and to imagine adventures past, as well as to undertake adventures present. It reeks of history, and the lobby of the hotel is filled with framed clippings, old photos, and artifacts that graphically describe the exciting times when America and Britain confronted each other as well as the later formation of John McMillan's empire and its days of glory. The legacy of bright flowers in formal gardens, old vine-covered buildings, and gaily bedecked yachts and flags all contribute to sharp memories of times past.

These intangibles are the most memorable and possibly the best part of the resort, but they are by no means all it has to offer. A fine stable of horses is maintained for trail rides. Two good concrete tennis courts (make reservations in advance if you can) and a large outdoor heated pool occupy the center of a big grassy area below the cottages. There is clam raking to be done, and fishing is good all around Henry Island across from the harbor (rental boats and tackle are available at the gas dock). Bicycling for exercise and as a means of exploring points of interest, such as the old English and American camps of Pig War days, is increasingly popular. And not to be missed at some point in the visit is a trip to the Whale Museum in Friday Harbor. Anyone not already a whale fan will be one for sure after seeing this remarkable collection.

Back at the resort, everything stops exactly at sundown when the "colors" ceremony takes place. Then, after the last flag comes down, live entertainment commences in the pavilion. Music floats out over the harbor and docks, and boaters drift from craft to craft and up to the pavilion to dance or to sit on the benches overlooking the scene and discuss their next cruise and the plans for tomorrow.

Dining

Roche Harbor Inn, next to the hotel, was once the home of John S. McMillan, who founded the lime works, built the hotel, and owned the town. Now the old mansion houses the restaurant, the cocktail lounge, and the pavilion.

All summer the inn is a busy place, so dinner reservations are a necessity. The food is reliably excellent and chosen from a diversified menu that emphasizes seafood. Full use of a good salad bar is included with every entrée, and there is an extensive wine list. Most tables afford views of the harbor. All in all, it is difficult not to linger here, except when you see the line of people waiting anxiously to get in.

Breakfast and lunch are served in the dining room, but for a simple

Docks at Friday Harbor

breakfast, you can buy fresh doughnuts and coffee at a snack bar next to the hotel's gift shop.

After Labor Day the dining room opens only on weekends, and in November it closes down completely until March. Then guests staying at the hotel take the fifteen-minute drive to Friday Harbor, where there are a number of restaurants available. The Wild Hare, two blocks up the hill from the ferry on the main street of town, is the fanciest of these, with a supper club atmosphere and a reputation for elegant cuisine. The Turnagain, just opposite the ferry dock, also is always good. There are several smaller places to discover. Simmco Central, for example, is an interestingly appointed tavern that serves good food right at the bar and is worth a visit. For a gourmet experience on the island, however, everyone will tell you the place to go is the Duck Soup Inn. Overlooking a picturesque pond out in the country about halfway between Roche Harbor and Friday Harbor, it is not always open, so be sure to call before making your dinner plans.

Central
Getaways

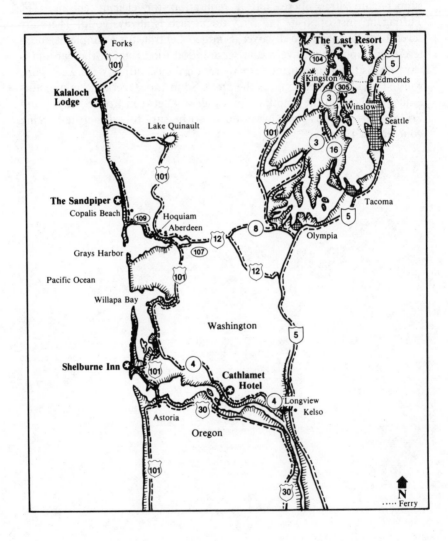

Forks
101
The Last Resort
104
5
Kingston
Edmonds
Kalaloch
Lodge
305
3
Winslow
Lake Quinault
101
Seattle
The Sandpiper
101
3
Copalis Beach
109
Hoquiam
16
Aberdeen
Tacoma
12
Grays Harbor
8
107
5
Pacific Ocean
101
Olympia
Willapa Bay
12
Washington
5
Shelburne Inn
4
101
Cathlamet
Hotel
4
Longview
Astoria
30
Kelso
Oregon
101
30
N
····· Ferry

Kalaloch Lodge

Distances:
From Seattle—170 miles; allow 3½ hours
From Portland—215 miles; allow 4½ hours
From Vancouver, B.C.—260 miles, plus ferry; allow 6 hours

Features:
Remote hideaway—35 miles from the nearest town—that is close to nature; every room and cottage faces the ocean; no telephones or television

Activities:
Beachcombing, winter-storm watching, crabbing, razor clamming, oystering, fishing, rain forest hiking; hunting in fall

Seasons:
Year-round

Rates:
$40 to $50 for two people in a Sea Crest House room; $30 to $36 in a lodge room; $40 to $58 in a cabin; three nights for the price of two on weekdays from 15 October to 1 May

Address:
Star Route 1, Box 1100, Forks, Washington 98331

Phone:
(206) 962-3411

Oceanside view of Kalaloch Lodge

On the whole Olympic Peninsula, only fifteen miles of U.S. 101 run alongside the Pacific beach. Above and below this stretch the ocean frontage is set aside as Indian reservations, while this one short section is included in the Olympic National Park. So for sixty-four miles, from the tiny settlement of Queets to the town of Forks, there are no houses, no stores, and no commercial activity, except, because it was here before the park was formed, Kalaloch Lodge.

The resort occupies a remarkably beautiful setting, right on the highway at the point where Kalaloch Creek flows into the sea. It includes a little store, the main lodge building, which contains the restaurant and lounge and eight apartment units, the new Sea Crest House with ten additional units, and a row of seventeen individual cabins on a low bluff above the beach.

Kalaloch is a long-established resort loved by generations of Washingtonians who set great store by its uniquely isolated location. Some of these people come back season after season; one couple has a lifetime reservation for the same cabin on the same date every year!

No tennis courts, golf courses, swimming pools, game rooms, telephones, or television sets impinge on the tranquility of this resort. People come for just three reasons: to enjoy the beach, to hunt or fish, or to escape the world and relax.

Routes and Distances

The drive to Kalaloch from any of our major cities is generally pleasant, and the lodge is easy to find. From Seattle or Portland go to Aberdeen and then north on U.S. 101, which leads directly to the lodge, seventy miles away. The Olympic Peninsula is lumber country, and the abundance of logging trucks and the speed at which they travel on this narrow highway can be unnerving, but relax: the drivers know their business and pilot the big rigs more safely than their size and speed first seem to indicate.

For those leaving home in the morning, a pleasant luncheon stop is the Lake Quinault Lodge, thirty-five miles south of Kalaloch and just two miles off the highway at a well-marked junction. There you will find a fine restaurant in a historic inn, well worth a visit.

Vancouverites can drive via Seattle to Aberdeen, but a shorter, more interesting route is to turn off Interstate 5 at Burlington and follow Washington 20 south through Whidbey Island to the Keystone ferry, which crosses Puget Sound to Port Townsend. From Port Townsend, get on U.S. 101 and drive west toward Port Angeles and Forks, approaching Kalaloch from the north.

Accommodations

Due to its venerable age, Kalaloch is made up of different structures built at different times and therefore quite at variance in appearance and appointments. The main lodge burned down a number of years ago and was rebuilt on exactly the same site. Now there are new owners with an ambitious plan to gradually remodel and modernize the entire resort, so more changes can be expected in the years ahead.

The eight rooms upstairs in the lodge are the least pretentious of all the accommodations (although they are bright and cheerful) and therefore are the least expensive. Only four of these have an ocean view, so specify a room on the view side if the lodge rooms are your choice. At the farther end of the resort complex, among a grove of wind-shaped trees, is the much newer Sea Crest House. Each of its ten rooms is comfortable and spacious; all have fireplaces and large picture windows and decks that face the ocean. Three units in this building are two-bedroom suites that can accommodate four to six people. These are appropriate for families or two couples traveling together if they do not mind sharing a single bath.

The seventeen cabins, however, are Kalaloch's main attraction. They are set in a semicircular pattern along the bluff and most have spectacular views and easy access to the beach. All have kitchenettes for those who want to hole up and do their own cooking, but cooking and eating utensils are not provided so you must remember to bring your own. Groceries are available at the little store on the grounds. Four of the

Cabin overlooking beach at Kalaloch

newest cabins have fireplaces and are large enough to accommodate four or more people very comfortably, making the cost per person extremely low for couples traveling together. A special attraction for pet owners is that for a small additional fee Kalaloch permits pets to accompany their owners in the cabin area.

Activities

Directly outside the cabin doors at Kalaloch, the wild beach stretches seven and a half miles in both directions, providing visitors with unexcelled razor clamming, beachcombing, jogging, and walking possibilities. It may seem strange that a person could walk all day and count it a success to find one little glass ball, but to a dedicated beachcomber such a find makes an exciting visit, and this is the best beach in Washington for finding Japanese floats, strange shapes of drift-wood and agates and jaspers in the rough.

For fishermen, there are many fine steelheading streams nearby, in-cluding the Kalaloch itself, and in summer season trout come in on the surf, along with the famous annual silver-smelt run. Dungeness crab and rock oysters can be collected in the tide pools by those who know how, and the Indian term *kalaloch* is said to translate into "lots of clams," which is word enough about the razor-clamming prospects.

During the fall elk season, the lodge is headquarters for hunters seeking big trophies. The rest of the year camera buffs take over to stalk the rain forest trails, where Roosevelt elk are frequently seen, sometimes quite close to the lodge itself.

The majority of visitors, though, come to Kalaloch for rest and relaxation. Here you can take a cabin for weeks in summer or a fireplace room for just a few days in winter and in either case enjoy a haven away-from-it-all that would be difficult to match.

Dining

The lodge is the sole eating facility for miles around, so in spite of its remoteness there is usually a bustle of activity, especially in the coffee shop, which serves as a meeting place for Park Service people and local residents who come by for lunch or coffee and conversation.

Perhaps the most charming part of the resort is the dining room, perched close to the low bluff and commanding a delightful view of the creek where it emerges from the forest and winds through a tangle of driftwood to the ocean. Three meals a day are served all year in the din-

Confluence of Kalaloch Creek and Pacific Ocean

ing room. At dinner time it can fill up unexpectedly, so it is advisable to obtain dinner reservations on arrival at the lodge. The menu appropriately emphasizes seafood, with a good selection of oysters, scallops, prawns, and baked salmon as well as combination dishes of steak and seafood. Two specialities are especially good: "Steak Oscar," which is a tender filet cooked to order, covered with crabmeat and asparagus spears, and loaded with béarnaise sauce; and a dish made from jumbo prawns stuffed with crab, covered with Parmesan cheese, and baked in butter and white wine. Selected Washington and California wines are served in the dining room, as well as cocktails from the Whaler's Lounge upstairs.

The Sandpiper

Distances:
> From Seattle—131 miles; allow 2¾ hours
> From Portland—176 miles; allow 3½ hours
> From Vancouver, B.C.—276 miles; allow 6 hours

Features:
> Comfortable modern apartments nestled in a woodsy setting on the beach; no restaurant or sport facilities

Activities:
> Walking, sunbathing, clamming, ocean watching

Seasons:
> Year-round

Rates:
> $37 to $45 for two people in a "beach house"; $27.50 and up in a cottage; 20% discount on winter weekdays

Address:
> P.O. Box A, Pacific Beach, Washington 98571

Phone:
> (206) 276-4580

Condominium units at Sandpiper face the beach

Perhaps more than most resorts in this book, the Sandpiper is a place to go to engineer an abrupt change of pace and escape from life's ordinary sights, sounds, and pressures. Some who like golf go on vacation to play more golf, and others who like tennis go someplace where they can get on the courts all day, but you go to the Sandpiper if you want to cut off the regular routines and forget about the world for a while. Even a newspaper is hard to come by here, and you can deliberately hold the march of time at bay.

The Sandpiper's three main buildings are relatively new, set all by themselves a mile and a half south of the little town of Pacific Beach and as close to the ocean as the architects dared pour their foundations. The bright, clean design, excellent maintenance by its owners, and closeness to many major Northwest cities are features that make this an ideal, out-of-the-ordinary getaway destination. It is exactly the fact that there is no restaurant, bar, or organized entertainment facilities that sets the Sandpiper apart, and indeed, for anyone whose objective is a peaceful time, these very lacks are its major asset.

Routes and Distances

From Portland, Seattle, or Vancouver, drive to Aberdeen-Hoquiam and get on Washington 109, which skirts Grays Harbor and leads to Copalis Beach. The resort is five and a half miles north of Copalis Beach on the ocean side of the road.

Accommodations

The core of the resort is two two-story "beach houses," which rise steeply out of the sands and nestle into an evergreen-studded bank in a manner that would delight any ecologist. In addition, there are five individual cottages, all of different size, shape, age, and capacity, scattered along the beach, as well as the weathered building where the owners live and keep their gift shop and office and the pottery studio.

All of the apartments in the beach houses are comfortably furnished and have modern kitchens and private, covered decks oriented to a 180-degree view of the ocean. All but two have fireplaces. The top-floor units have vaulted ceilings with heavy beams, adding to the sense of spaciousness and accentuating the breadth of the view from the picture windows. Couples will be perfectly comfortable in the studio apartments, which have pull-down queen-size beds and two couches. For a slightly higher rate they can have a corner one-bedroom unit, which is more spacious and a good bargain.

The cottages are not as new and therefore not as slick as the beach house units, but they accordingly offer the most modestly priced accommodations. All but one of the cottages have fireplaces.

Unlike so many resorts, pets are welcome here if they are kept under supervision and not left alone in the rooms. There is a small fee for such

Ocean view from Sandpiper condominium

additional guests, with the important exception that *all* dachshunds are the cordially invited, free guests of Barney, the resident dog at the Sandpiper.

Activities

People come to the beach for many different reasons, but first and foremost is to find peace and quiet and get away from it all. Those who come to the Sandpiper are able to do this particularly well. The level beach is just yards from the buildings. The ocean's roar is background music to everything you do, and the kitchen facilities provided in each unit make it unnecessary to dress and go out for breakfast or lunch, or even dinner, unless that is what you want to do. There are no telephones or television sets, and without the newspaper you can forget the world's bad news; just sit on your private deck and read and watch the waves, or go out to the beach and dig clams or walk for miles.

Clammers can buy their licenses and rent shovels right at the front desk and then clean their catch in a little house that has sinks and hot water for that purpose and is situated just off the beach.

In the lobby the management provides a well-stocked lending library of paperback books and a little gift shop, which has a reputation as one of the best-stocked shops on the coast. Pottery is the item for which it is best known. Pots are "thrown" by two local artists, Lorene Spencer and Reni Moriarity, in an adjoining studio right on the site, where guests can

Walking the beach at low tide

watch them working at their wheels. Betty Winders, a co-owner of the Sandpiper, does the final decorating and glazing. She says that sometimes people insist on placing orders while the pots are still too hot to touch for fear that if they wait until the pots cool someone else might come along and claim them!

Dining

People who come to the Sandpiper prepared to do their own cooking will find it a painless maneuver in the well-equipped kitchenettes. Most plan ahead for all breakfasts and lunches and perhaps bring the makings for a simple dinner such as steak and salad to tide them over until they can dig some clams and enjoy the ocean's bounty. Eating on the deck right over the Pacific is always a pleasant experience during nice weather.

For those who are outwitted by fast-digging clams or simply don't like to cook on vacation, there is a pleasant alternative. The Ocean Crest Dinner House is just a few miles north on Highway 109 and sits on a high bluff overlooking the surf, which at night is illuminated dramatically with carefully concealed spotlights. This is rightfully known as one of the finest restaurants on the Washington coast, and it is always worth going a little out of the way to have dinner here. The Ocean Crest is still operated by members of the Curtright family, who started it and have built a tradition of gourmet food and fine service over many years. The menu is long and delightful and quite reasonably priced, and each dinner always commences with razor-clam chowder and a green salad. Anyone on a diet should be wary indeed of the elegant homemade grasshopper pie and cheesecake offered at the end of the meal.

Shelburne Inn

Distances:

From Seattle—175 miles; allow 3½ hours

From Portland—115 miles; allow 2¼ hours

From Vancouver, B.C.—320 miles; allow 7 hours

Features:

An authentic example of 1890s inn-keeping style; especially gracious hospitality amongst a wealth of antique furnishings; located in a quiet, interesting beachside village

Activities:

Beach walking and driving, jetty scrambling, bird-watching, clamming, salmon fishing, picnicking, looking at old cottages and life-styles

Seasons:

Year-round

Rates:

$22 to $26 for two people

Address:

P.O. Box 250, Seaview, Washington 98644

Phone:

(206) 642-2442

Shelburne Inn on main street of Seaview

Seaview, like so many oceanfront towns, is spread out string-bean fashion along a single avenue running parallel to the beach. On a corner of this main thoroughfare sits the Shelburne Inn. Enclosed by a white picket fence, it looks very much as it did almost a century ago, in 1896, when Charles Beaver moved his fine old Victorian house across the street—with the help of a team of horses—and joined it to a similar building to create the inn.

It is hard to believe that in those days, before the long north jetty was built at the mouth of the Columbia, the ocean came right to the inn's door. The summer boarders, mostly Portlanders who came down the river on steamers to spend the season, could step right out on the beach to rake crabs, dig clams, and swim in the surf. Now, over the years since the completion of the jetty, the ocean currents have been redirected and the shoreline has retreated at least a half mile from its old location. But even though it has lost its waterfront, the Shelburne retains its charm. The friendly old building, which has been placed on the National Register of Historic Places, is as comfortable as can be, in spite of rolling floors and creaking doors, and it is doubtful that any of the innkeepers of the past could have been more hospitable than David and Laurie Campiche, the young couple who run the inn today and extend so many thoughtful niceties to provide their guests with a memorable experience.

Routes and Distances

From Portland either take U.S. 30 to Astoria and then U.S. 101 north to Seaview, or cross to Washington on Interstate 5, drive to Kelso, and from there take Washington 4 to its intersection with 101 at the coast. Seaview is fifteen miles south on 101. The two routes are approximately equal in mileage, and both provide easy, scenic driving.

From Vancouver or Seattle take I-5 south to Olympia, then U.S. 12 toward Aberdeen, but before arriving at Aberdeen turn right on Washington 107 at Montesano, cut across to 101, and drive south for sixty-two miles to Seaview. Like the route from Portland, this is also an easy, relaxing drive.

From Raymond south, you are in oyster country. Scattered along the shores of Willapa Bay are the oyster fisheries, easily recognized by their great piles of bleached white shells. A good way to sample their product is to plan a luncheon stop at Boondocks in South Bend, two and a half hours out of Seattle. Hard to miss because of its distinctive bright blue paint, the restaurant is located on the Willapa River at the head of the bay. Diners can look out over commercial fishing vessels tied alongside as they eat their meal. Try the "Hangtown Fry," a delectable combination of pan-fried oysters and scrambled eggs, for a pleasant treat.

Accommodations

Many of the antiques that practically fill this inn to overflowing are imported from England, and most of them are for sale—an interesting secondary enterprise of the proprietors. All of the fifteen bedrooms are furnished accordingly, with pieces from the late nineteenth and early twentieth centuries. Each room has its own individuality, with bed frames ranging from brass to ornately carved wood, along with a surprising variety of dressers, washstands, lamps, and miscellaneous old decorations. But there is a price to pay for all this charm. Though each room has a washbasin, it is "down the hall" to one of the five commonly shared bathrooms. Considering the mood of the inn and the modest tariffs charged, however, it is a small price indeed.

Activities

The Long Beach Peninsula, as the name implies, has the longest, straightest, and possibly widest stretch of beach on the West Coast. From Seaview north, automobile traffic is allowed on the beach, and beach driving is a popular way to see the scenery and get to the best clamming grounds. (Drivers should go slowly and stay on the hard sand above the wet-line to avoid injuring clams, which stay close to the surface in the wet areas.)

The favorite beach for walkers and picnickers, however, is a three-

Oyster-processing plant in Oysterville

mile-long, driftwood-laden section of protected "wild" beach on which no automobiles or any kind of development is permitted. This stretch is just above the north jetty with access through Fort Canby, ten minutes south of Seaview. The jetty itself is a half-mile-long boulder pile pointing like a finger out to sea. It makes an interesting rock scramble, and from its end seals and sea lions can sometimes be seen and photographed. Ship traffic in and out of the Columbia parades past the jetty's tip, and the city of Astoria is visible far away on the Oregon side of the river.

At Fort Canby you'll find an operating lighthouse set on green lawns and old gun emplacements that once guarded the mouth of the Columbia. For hikers, a 1.2-mile forest trail leads out to McKenzie Head. Good picnicking sites abound throughout this area.

When returning to the inn from Fort Canby, go by way of Ilwaco to see the boats and the cannery built on pilings over the water. In the summer salmon season, when the charter boats are operating, this town is alive with activity; during the rest of the year, it is a typically picturesque fishing village.

In the other direction, on the extreme north tip of the spit, there are more trails and picnic sites at Leadbetter Point State Park, a bird sanctuary much favored by nature lovers. On the way to the park, the road passes through the little communities of Nahcotta and Oysterville, which are worth inspecting. Oysterville has a large, white oyster-processing plant where you can buy a supply of fresh, iced-down oysters to take home. Visitors are not permitted in the cannery itself, but it is possible to watch the line of shuckers at work through windows directly behind the processing conveyor.

Close to the inn itself it is fun to stroll the little-traveled back streets of Seaview where dozens of unusual old cottages and houses, many with yards and areaways decorated by artifacts from the sea, wait to be

Quiet inlet at Fort Canby

discovered. Those who want to explore a little farther afield should ask David Campiche for suggestions, inquiring particularly about a trip to Long Island, an unlogged, completely natural game preserve—and a beautiful picnic site—located close-by but accessible only by boat or canoe.

Dining

The dining area of the Shelburne is in what was the drawing room of the original Victorian house. Like everything else in the inn, it is furnished with antiques, its tables and chairs arranged along the lead-paned windows or around the free-standing iron fireplace. An old staircase leading down from the second floor adds to the nineteenth century charm.

At dinnertime guests make their choice of entrées from a blackboard that stands at the entrance of the room. Though limited in variety, the menu offers excellent selections, such as cod stuffed with crab, a jambalaya shrimp dish, or selections of tenderloin steak and chateaubriand. Soup and a fresh salad come with the dinner, and homemade desserts are available. The wine list is small but provides a good choice of wines to go with every dinner.

The hostess, Laurie Campiche, prepares lovely breakfasts for her guests. Fresh homemade croissants are often part of the menu, along with wild huckleberry jam, fruit, English-style coddled eggs, and a pot of steaming coffee.

Lunch is served Wednesday through Saturday, while on Sunday the feature is a big and sumptuous brunch. Mondays and Tuesdays guests are on their own—a good excuse to pack a picnic from the grocery just across the street and head out for the beach or woods.

The Last Resort

Distances:

>From Seattle—20 miles, plus ferry; allow 1¼ hours
>
>From Portland—195 miles, plus ferry; allow 4½ hours
>
>From Vancouver, B.C.—141 miles, plus ferry; allow 3½ hours

Features:

>Very small, tucked-out-of-the-way beach resort near Seattle; no restaurant and few of the other usual amenities, but a true hideaway

Activities:

>Beach walking, bird-watching, fishing, clamming, oystering, crabbing, swimming, picnicking, volleyball, winter-storm watching

Seasons:

>Year-round

Rates:

>$35 for two people in summer; $28 from September through May

Address:

>2546 Northeast Twin Spits Road, Hansville, Washington 98340

Phone:

>(206) 638-2358

Cabins at Last Resort on Hood Canal

The Last Resort is tiny, unostentatious, and utterly opposite to big, well-known resorts with elaborate facilities. It does have a swimming pool and a volleyball net; otherwise, it is just five little cabins and a house that the manager lives in set on a spit of beach at the end of a road. But it is only twenty minutes from the Kingston ferry landing and the closest to a big city of any of the resorts in this book, and from every cabin there are fine, peaceful views of water, mountains, sky, and distant headlands. It is a place to be lazy, to compose thoughts without interruption, to poke about the beach, and to sit in one of Puget Sound's few sun pockets and soak up the good warmth in summer or to storm-watch before a blazing fire in winter.

Routes and Distances

Cross Puget Sound on either the Seattle-Winslow or the Edmonds-Kingston ferry. Both run almost hourly every day of the year [call (206) 464-6400 for precise departure information]. From Kingston, go west on Washington 104 for one mile to a traffic light with signs indicating a right turn to the Hansville Recreation area. Take the right turn and drive nine more miles through Hansville, and continue to follow the same road for another two miles. It becomes Twin Spits Road and terminates at the Last Resort.

From Winslow, follow Washington 305 north. After crossing the Agate Pass Bridge, follow signs to Suquamish and then Kingston. At the junction with Washington 104, do not turn right toward Kingston. Instead, continue straight north toward Hansville, where the road becomes Twin Spits Road and terminates at the Last Resort.

Accommodations

The five little cabins at the Last Resort are arranged in a row and are much alike. Each has two bedrooms, a bathroom with shower, a spacious living area with a Fire-Vue fireplace-stove and plenty of wood, and a bright kitchenette. As is typical of most beach cabins, the furnishings are simple and utilitarian but comfortable, and the cabins have linoleum floors instead of rugs to make it easy to sweep out the sand. They are within easy access of the beach, and all share the same wide view of the juncture of Hood Canal and Puget Sound. The cabins are roomy for a couple and quite suitable for two couples if they do not mind sharing a bath.

For really large groups and families of six or eight or more, there is a house above the manager's quarters that has three bedrooms and a full kitchen and can be made available upon inquiry.

Activities

Handily, right next door to the Last Resort is a marine launch facility that also rents boats and motors. At low tide, clams and oysters can be taken on the resort's own beach, but there are better places across the canal. For an interesting experience, rent a boat for a half day to coincide with low tide and go over to the Hood Head Spit or into the coves behind Port Ludlow; either destination is only twenty or thirty minutes away by outboard. Ask the resort's manager and the boat launch people about precise locations to find shellfish, then bring the results back for shucking and cooking at your cabin. Besides oystering, salmon and cod fishing are always worth a try in this part of the sound. Two favorite spots where results usually are good are Point-No-Point just to the north, and Possession Point off Whidbey Island to the east, both only short runs from the resort.

Along the beaches long walks are possible in both directions, depending on the tide. The lower the tide, the farther you can go, although to completely traverse the more interesting northerly spit it is sometimes necessary to remove shoes and trousers and wade across a thigh-deep inlet that bars the way. Shells of every sort and agates of many colors abound on this walk, and the marine view is unsurpassed. In the other direction, to the left, you can go down the beach a mile and then take an indistinctly marked trail inland through a place known as the "nature conservancy," a nesting and breeding place for birds. The trail goes through marsh and woods, coming out to the main road, on which you take the walk back to the resort. Consult the manager about how to find the trail entrance.

Walking the sandy spit at Last Resort

The heated swimming pool has a concrete deck around it and lounge furniture on which to soak up the sun on nice days.

Thus there are things to do for the active, but without television, telephones, or disturbing traffic of any kind, the Last Resort always will be mainly a place to take a pile of unread books and unanswered correspondence and, between hikes and oystering expeditions, settle back to read, write, and dream a little.

Dining

Guests usually do their own cooking in the fully equipped little kitchens in their cabins. Although there is a small store in Hansville for forgotten items, you should plan to bring your own food and condiments. Next to the cabin's kitchen is a pleasant indoor eating area, but picnic tables directly outside the front door are more fun in fine weather. There also is a fire pit with two more tables within a hundred feet, next to the beach.

If you prefer to have dinner out, several little restaurants can be found in Hansville and Kingston. But for first-class dining and a real treat, allow a few extra minutes to drive the seventeen miles to Poulsbo. The Olympic Inn, which is easily found on the left side of the street in the main part of town, is as good as any of the top restaurants in either Seattle or Portland.

Picnicking on sandy beach at Last Resort

Cathlamet Hotel

Distances:

From Portland—74 miles; allow 1½ hours

From Seattle—153 miles; allow 3¼ hours

From Vancouver, B.C.—298 miles; allow 6 hours

Features:

Renovated, small 1920s hotel with superb dining in a sleepy riverside town

Activities:

Poking around Cathlamet, picnicking; tennis and golf nearby

Seasons:

Year-round

Rates:

$20 to $22 for two people; includes continental breakfast

Address:

67-69 Main Street, Cathlamet, Washington 98612

Phone:

(206) 795-8751 or (206) 795-3997

Entrance to Cathlamet Hotel

Cathlamet, a tiny, out-of-the-way town on the banks of the Columbia River, was a thriving fishing and logging center in the era when the river was the avenue of commerce, providing the sole means of transportation for everything that moved in and out of town. But today the big waterside cannery buildings stand weather-beaten and almost empty, used only for drying fish nets and miscellaneous storage, and the loggers have long since faded into the past.

The principal street in Cathlamet is just one block long, with a short side lane running down to the waterfront docks and cannery. Right in the middle of the block on the main street and directly across from a stately, old-style county courthouse is the Cathlamet Hotel, which dates back to the 1920s, and Pierre's Restaurant alongside it to the west. It is these two buildings, recently renovated and presently operated by a charming family, that have put Cathlamet back on the map. Because of them the sleepy little town has been rediscovered as a place to "weekend" and get away from it all. The ingredients are all there: a romantic and nostalgic small hotel, a fine restaurant where dining can consume an entire evening, and an area steeped in history and full of things to explore.

But there is no doubt that dining is the highlight of the trip to Cathlamet. Every night, besides the hotel guests, the restaurant is filled with people who have journeyed by car or boat all the way from Portland and Astoria to enjoy one of Pierre's famous repasts—a decisive indication of how well and how far his reputation has spread.

Routes and Distances

During the boating season, many visitors come by boat to Cathlamet, where they put in at the Elochoman Marina, located in a cozy harbor an easy walking distance from town. This is, in fact, the last safe harbor between Portland and Astoria. For those making the trip downriver, it is, therefore, an attractive place to stop for fuel and supplies, as well as for dinner or to spend the night.

By automobile, Cathlamet is twenty-five miles west of Longview on the pretty riverside highway, Washington 4. From Seattle or Vancouver come down Interstate 5 almost to Kelso and watch for a well-marked exit onto 4. From Portland drive north on I-5 to Kelso and west on 4 from there to Cathlamet, or take U.S. 30 through Saint Helens to Westport. Then cross the Columbia to Puget Island on the little ferry, which leaves more or less on an hourly schedule, and then drive over the bridge from there to Cathlamet.

Accommodations

What do you do when you have ten kids and don't want to raise them in Chicago? Move to Cathlamet, of course, buy a run-down old hotel, and start a family enterprise destined to become the delight of hideaway seekers.

With the help of their children, Pierre Pype and his wife, Claire, spent almost a year renovating the sixty-year-old Cathlamet Hotel, which, although threadbare and neglected, was discovered to be of basically sound construction. The result of their hard work was the creation of twelve cheerful units, brightly wallpapered and newly carpeted but in keeping with the spirit of the times when the hotel was built. There are no television sets or telephones in these little rooms, and much of the furniture is from the original 1920s-vintage hotel, with some additional antiques purchased to fill in. All of the rooms are on the second floor; most look out on the main street and have old-fashioned double-hung windows, putting one in direct contact with the mingled noises of birds chirping and motors starting up as the town comes to life in the morning.

Two of the rooms have their own private baths, some adjoining rooms share a bath between, and the other rooms necessitate a trip to the fancifully decorated "washrooms" down the hall. All the rooms are so

Waterfront scene in Cathlamet

modestly priced, however, that whichever one you get, you can't help but think you are getting a bargain.

The hotel has a spacious lobby on the upper level in which guests are invited to relax with a book or socialize with friends. It is a pleasant area with bright red carpeting and white wicker furniture and filled with souvenirs and memorabilia of days gone by in Wahkiakum County.

A notable weekend plan must be mentioned. It is called the "honeymoon special," but it doesn't matter which "honeymoon" you are enjoying. For the attractive price of eighty-nine dollars, a couple can have two nights at the hotel, two dinners at Pierre's, and a special Sunday champagne brunch.

Activities

For city people the most enjoyable activity is simply seeing how people live in this small town—by strolling past the stores and churches, going down to the marina, investigating the old cannery buildings, poking around on the riverfront, and making a nostalgic visit to the informal little Wahkiakum County Museum a block from the hotel. It is jammed with homey artifacts from Cathlamet's days of glory, and will give you a good understanding of its fascinating past as well as its present.

For photographers who like to find and capture atmosphere and detail, Cathlamet and the vicinity are a little paradise, full of such scenes as weather-beaten siding with a shutter hanging on one hinge, a vintage fire truck slowly being overgrown by weeds, fishing boats tied among houseboats and rickety docks on a slough, or an old covered bridge.

Both up and down the river, picnickers can find sites for watching activity on the water. Or across the bridge on Puget Island, they can find, with a little searching, an isolated sandy beach on which to spread out their lunch. On a fine day they might even have lunch on a bench by the ferry landing while observing the picturesque little ferry plying back and forth to Oregon.

For more vigorous sport, Cathlamet has four public tennis courts, two at the school and two in a pretty, wooded park on Columbia Street, a half mile up the hill from the hotel. About a mile to the east just off the highway is a sporty little nine-hole golf course, the Skyline Golf Links, where it is hardly ever necessary to wait to tee off.

Dining

Many people wonder how the tiny town of Cathlamet came to have such a fine restaurant as Pierre's. The answer is simple. The Pype family found, after putting so much energy into restoring the hotel, that they needed a restaurant, too, because the only other restaurant in town closed at six in the evening—not very suitable for people looking for a leisurely weekend. Fortunately, just about that time the old house next door was scheduled for the wrecker's ball, and the Pypes quickly bought the place and once more began a huge restoration job.

Gingerbread was added to the facade. The exterior was painted bright tomato red with white trim. The outer rooms, both upstairs and down, were turned into intimate little dining alcoves. The old parlors and living room were remodeled, equipped with an old pot-bellied stove and giant old-fashioned ceiling fans, and filled with authentic 1920 furniture.

Just as they worked to make the decor charming, the Pypes outdid themselves in finding and training good chefs and designing a fine menu. The food, in short, is excellent, and it is served in a relaxed atmosphere in which guests are expected to dally a couple of hours over dinner. The wine list is especially extensive; Pierre is an expert on wines and has built an inventory of almost fifteen hundred European and domestic brands.

It should be noted that in spite of the suggestibility of its name, Pierre's is not a French restaurant but was simply named for the owner. Its specialties are carefully aged beef selections, of which Pierre is particularly proud, and a variety of seafood items. Notable among the seafoods is "Shrimp de Johnge," a recipe invented and made famous by Pierre's great uncle, who was a restaurateur in Chicago.

Each morning the hotel serves all guests a continental breakfast. It can be enjoyed in bed, in the room, or out in the bright second-floor lobby, which is flooded with morning sunlight from the skylight above. A pot of steaming coffee, a generous glass of orange juice, hot rolls, and a slice of melon go a long way to start your day on an upbeat note. For lunch you are on your own, but be advised to leave plenty of room for dinner at Pierre's in the evening!

Gingerbread facade of Pierre's Restaurant

East-Central
Getaways

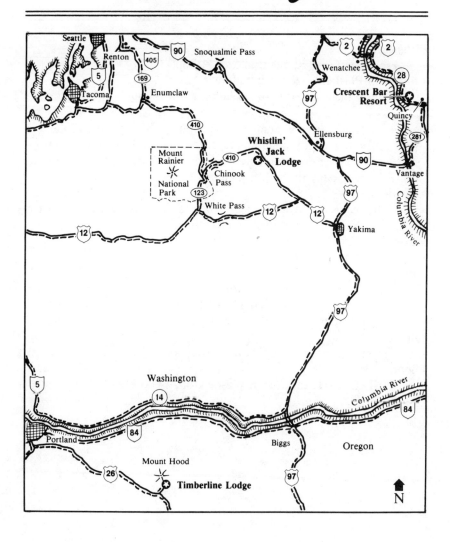

Crescent Bar Resort

Distances:
From Seattle—170 miles; allow 3¼ hours
From Portland—280 miles; allow 6 hours
From Vancouver, B.C.—285 miles; allow 6 hours

Features:
An "Island in the Sun" at Wanapum Lake on the Columbia River; eighty condominium units in a still-growing development; temperature averages seventy degrees, with little rain, from May through September

Activities:
Golf, tennis, volleyball, water-skiing, swimming, outdoor Jacuzzi; alpine skiing nearby; bird hunting in fall

Seasons:
Year-round, but winter activities are limited

Rates:
$40 for studio units, $45 for one-bedroom units, $55 for two-bedroom units; winter ski packages are available, including transportation from Seattle and to the ski area and all meals

Address:
Crescent Bar Resort, Quincy, Washington 98848

Phone:
(509) 787-1511; toll free in Washington, 1-800-572-4528

Free-form pool is center of activity at Crescent Bar

Crescent Bar was originally a wide, low shelf of land hedged by the Columbia River on one side and a towering row of basalt cliffs on the other. In the days when the Columbia was the main artery of commerce into central Washington, steamboats plied up and down the river; the area around the bar became a fairly thriving community because it afforded good landing places for the steamers. All that stopped abruptly when the first dams were built, blocking navigation on the river. The bar became isolated and forgotten—just a green speck with a few orchards in an otherwise dry landscape. Then a dozen years ago another dam, the Wanapum, was built near Vantage, and the water backing up behind it shrank the bar into a 260-acre island.

From early spring through late fall the sun shines incessantly in this region; clouds are rare and rain practically nonexistent. But the water rights established by the early orchardists permit extensive irrigation, and the bar was seen by a visionary developer as a potential oasis in a sunny climate not far from Puget Sound's gray weather and an ideal place for a resort.

The development plan that emerged called for a self-contained community centered around privately owned condominiums that would be available for rent to the public when not occupied by the owners. A golf course, tennis courts, swimming beaches, private home sites, a first-class restaurant, a marina, a travel-trailer park, a skeet range, and many other amenities would surround the condominiums.

Now, several years later, much of this plan has been realized, but it is not complete; in fact, the plan keeps growing as new projects are added. Completion of the development is therefore some time away; nevertheless, the main elements necessary for pleasant vacationing are already there, and although the name Crescent Bar is not yet well known, word about it is spreading and its popularity is on the upswing. New visitors will understand why and will find it easy to imagine that this will someday become one of Washington's most popular resorts.

Routes and Distances

From Seattle drive over Snoqualmie Pass on Interstate 90, crossing the Columbia at Vantage. Continue on I-90 to George, Washington (if you are hungry you can eat there, quite appropriately, at Martha's Place) and turn north on Washington 281 to Quincy. From Quincy take Washington 28 toward Wenatchee for seven miles to the well-marked Crescent Bar entry road. An alternate route from Seattle is to take U.S. 2 over Stevens Pass. After crossing the Columbia, turn south on Washington 28 toward East Wenatchee and drive twenty-three miles along the river to the resort.

From Vancouver drive to Everett, turn east on U.S. 2, and continue as directed above.

From Portland drive to Yakima and continue north on U.S. 97 for thirty-four miles to the junction with Interstate 90. Turn east on I-90 and proceed to Vantage and Quincy according to the Seattle instructions.

Accommodations

Crescent Bar's eighty condominium units are arranged to form a private, enclosed compound around a manicured lawn and a spectacular free-form pool. All of the architecture is of classic Mediterranean style, with white plaster facades and red tile roofs set in impressive contrast to the stark cliffs beyond.

Rental units are available in three floor plans. The smallest are studios with a main living-dining area and a bedroom alcove. Next are one-bedroom units that have a separate bedroom as well as a hide-a-bed in the living room. Finally, there are two-bedroom units, which are identical in floor plan to those with one bedroom but in addition have a large loft containing two double beds.

All units have a single bathroom and a small kitchenette complete with cooking and eating utensils. Because each of the eighty units has been furnished and equipped by its individual owner, the type of decor differs from unit to unit. Some units, therefore, are more lavish than others, but all are comfortable. After people become familiar with the resort they can request specific units when making their reservations.

Massive bluffs shelter Crescent Bar's tennis courts

Activities

The swimming pool is the center of attraction at Crescent Bar. Some people spend whole days there; others come back to it after they have enjoyed other activities. The water temperature is carefully controlled to encourage frequent use, and the pool, unlike most public ones, has a good, flexible diving board, which divers will appreciate. The pool is divided into two sections that separate small children from the adults, and near one end is a whirlpool spa that is kept hot year-round.

The golf course is a par-thirty-six nine-holer that is very flat and has a good view of the Columbia from the fairways. The first tee is less than 100 yards from the condominiums, right outside the pro shop, where rental clubs, carts, and pull carts are available. A golf professional is on hand for lessons, and there is a driving range and putting green for those who want to practice. (Late in the season an extra hazard may appear in the form of occasional elk grazing in the rough. They see the grass from their dry range beyond the river and sometimes swim across to it. Or if not elk, there may be Canada geese, also attracted by the green grass, on the course.)

The social center and general meeting place at Crescent Bar is "The Store," which also contains the golf and tennis shops. Across the street are the tennis courts: four first-class, hard-surfaced, Laykold-type

Water-skiing on smooth surface of Wanapum Lake

courts, with a teaching professional who oversees scheduling, gives lessons, and, in summer, holds tennis camps. Beyond the courts is a five-acre lawn containing a baseball field, a volleyball court, and a wide assortment of swings, jungle gyms, and other playground equipment. Across the lawn, on the back side of the island, is a wide sand beach and the water-ski area. This is a lee shore with additional shelter from the tall cliffs, which helps keep the water flat, making it especially good for skiing—so good, in fact, that more than a half dozen official water-ski tournaments are held here every summer. The resort provides a launching ramp and gassing facilities for skiers who bring in their own boats.

During the fall, when bird-hunting season starts, Crescent Bar is a good hunting headquarters. The surrounding country is known for its abundant supply of chukars, Chinese pheasant, dove, and quail, and, not far away, the Potholes Reservoir affords some of the best duck and goose hunting in the state.

In winter, when reservations are easy to make, the resort is a comfortable place to stay while skiing Mission Ridge. On this side of the mountains, as compared with the west side, the snow is drier and more reliable, the lift lines shorter, and the traffic up to the ski area thinner, all of which makes a short midwinter ski vacation in Eastern Washington very enjoyable.

Dining

At the present stage of development there is no full scale restaurant at the resort, although having one built is a high priority (it might even be in operation by the time this book goes to print). But meanwhile there is just the little store on the premises with its breakfast and sandwich bar for light meals.

For dinners, therefore, it is advisable to come prepared to use the kitchenette in your apartment. Every unit also has a deck or patio where, if you bring a small portable barbecue along, steaks and hamburgers can be prepared outdoors. The store has a limited supply of canned goods, frozen meats, and beer and wine, but no fresh produce. Plan ahead, therefore, and bring food from home or stock up in Quincy or Wenatchee when passing through.

Should you prefer not to cook, you will have to drive twenty-four miles to Wenatchee, where there are several restaurants, or ten miles to Quincy. The best restaurants in Wenatchee are Coveys and the Chieftan, for standard fare, and David Brown's for Mexican food. In Quincy, the Turf cooks passable steaks.

Whistlin' Jack Lodge

Distances:
> From Seattle—110 miles; allow 2½ hours
> From Portland—195 miles; allow 4 hours
> From Vancouver, B.C.—255 miles; allow 5½ hours

Features:
> A fine riverfront dining room in an unexpected location: the last outpost between Yakima and Mount Rainier on the Chinook Pass Highway; rustic cabin accommodations and modern motel units overlooking the Naches River; solitude on the edge of the wilderness

Activities:
> Fishing and hunting in season, hiking, cross-country skiing, snowmobiling, horsepack trips, trail riding

Seasons:
> Year-round

Rates:
> $34 to $38 for two people in a motel unit, $45 to $50 for two to four people in a cottage

Address:
> 18936 Highway 410, Naches, Washington 98937

Phone:
> (509) 658-2433

Whistlin' Jack Lodge on the banks of the Naches River

Whistlin' Jack Lodge is located deep in the Cascades on the east side of Chinook Pass. In winter, when snows close the pass, most visitors are "east-siders" from the Yakima area, just forty-five minutes away. In summer, it is a different story. Once the snows melt and the passes are open, vacationers from all directions take to the mountains. Many cross Chinook Pass to enjoy the indescribable scenic beauty and the abundant recreational opportunities in the area, and not a few end up at this little lodge standing all by itself between the highway and the banks of the Naches River.

The "Whistling Jack" is a species of marmot that inhabits rocky slopes in this part of the high Cascades and emits a sharp, piercing whistle when startled. The Williams family adopted the name for the lodge when they acquired it in 1957. Doug Williams, the present owner, says he frowns on referring to his place as a resort: "After all, what we do is provide pleasant rooms overlooking the river and excellent meals, and we don't try to have a lot of activities and recreational facilities." But what he doesn't say is that, for many, this is the perfect starting point and home base for fishing, hiking, and pack trips into a vast area of mountains, rivers, streams, high lakes, and endless forests that extends in every direction. For addicts of golf, tennis, boating, and bicycling, Whistlin' Jack Lodge is not the place to go—unless they are seeking a cure for their addiction. But in that case it could be the best choice they ever made.

Routes and Distances

From Vancouver or Seattle drive south to Enumclaw and take Washington 410 into Mount Rainier National Park and across Chinook Pass. Continue on 410 for thirty-one miles to Cliffdell, which will be the first sign of civilization encountered since entering the park. Whistlin' Jack is the only thing in Cliffdell; you can't miss it.

From November until spring, when the pass is closed, it is necessary to take Cayuse Pass (Washington 123) out of the park to U.S. 12, which crosses White Pass en route to Yakima. Follow 12 for forty-five miles to its intersection with 410, where you turn left and go north twenty more miles to Cliffdell.

From Portland take Interstate 5 north to the intersection with U.S. 12 at Mary's Corner and follow 12, as above, across White Pass to 410 and Cliffdell.

Whether it is winter or summer, from the park entrance all the way to the lodge these routes are tremendously scenic drives with one spectacular view after another of Mount Rainier and the inner Cascade Mountains.

Accommodations

Connected to the lodge by a breezeway is a two-story building containing Whistlin' Jack's newest sleeping quarters. It has eight cheerful

Cabin in the woods at Whistlin' Jack

rooms, all identical, each with a large bedroom with two double beds, a dressing room, a bath, and a fine view overlooking the beautiful river directly below.

Farther from the lodge, scattered in a wooded area, are five roomy, plainly furnished cottages, some of which date back a number of years. These vary in size and shape, but all have kitchens and fireplaces and most have two bedrooms. Groups of hunters and fishermen like the cabins, and they work out nicely for families with children, but they are not well suited for two couples because the entry to the bath is through one of the bedrooms. The kitchens have a breakfast bar and dining alcove with table and chairs, but no utensils are provided, perhaps because of problems in the past. The lodge supplies a kit of cooking and eating equipment on request for a five-dollar deposit, which is returned when the equipment is brought back.

At night, there is little traffic—and no freight trucks—on the highway. An immense quiet descends on the area, and the lulling undertone of the river emphasizes the stillness. You know then that you are deep in the woods, and sleep comes easily.

Activities

The Whistlin' Jack's corral and wrangler Bob Henry's quarters are along the road, not over fifty yards from the lodge. Henry keeps his horses on pasture six miles away, bringing them up to the corral the night before a ride is scheduled. He takes groups on day rides or overnighters on a flexible schedule and provides all the gear and food; people need to bring only personal items, clothing, and a sleeping bag. The corral operates from June through October, packing guests into the mountains for fishing at remote lakes or sight-seeing, or hunting in the high country in the fall. If there are some who want to bring their own riding horses and camping equipment, that is fine; Henry will supply a pack animal and act as guide and packer. To make arrangements and reservations for these increasingly popular trips, call the lodge as early as possible. Rates are surprisingly reasonable, and for a great many people this is a rare opportunity to find out what an overnight pack trip into the mountains is like and, in any event, to have a long-remembered experience.

Since Whistlin' Jack has no facilities for other sport activities, it appeals mostly to those who like to find things to do on their own. Exploring Boulder Cave is one of these; it is close-by and provides a ruggedly beautiful sample of the scenery throughout the whole area. To get to the cave, cross the Naches on a bridge a quarter mile above the lodge and drive a mile on a Forest Service road, following the river to a parking area where a well-marked trail begins. Take the trail for a half mile through woods and into a precipitous ravine that ends at a waterfall. One hundred yards to the left of the waterfall is the cave mouth. The tunnellike cave is pitch black inside; a flashlight is necessary. Pick your way along the

Guided trail ride

underground stream that originally formed the cave, and you will come out, finally, in a branch of the ravine from which you started.

The same Forest Service road leading to the cave follows the river for miles in both directions and is fairly flat and almost completely devoid of auto traffic, making it ideal for jogging and walking in summer and cross-country skiing in winter.

Back in the direction of Chinook Pass is Raven Roost, a lookout that provides unusual views of Mount Rainier and its surrounding geography and is accessible by auto. In the pass itself, there are dozens of hiking and easy climbing opportunities. You can drive to the pass from the lodge in a half hour, climb Naches Peak, for example, or take the trail down to Dewey Lake, and be back from either in time for dinner.

Dining

In the dining room, tables are arranged along the window wall that faces the Naches River, and a surprising first item on the menu is an invitation to guests to feel free to open the screened windows and let in the river's sounds and breezes, should they feel so inclined. And because the river is almost an integral part of the dining room, those extra perceptions enhance the enjoyment of this unusual place. The second thing on the menu to catch the eye is the announcement of the house specialty: a fresh twelve-to-fourteen-inch trout, fried to a delicate brown. Should you order this, it will arrive attractively garnished and, after you have had a suitable chance to admire its appearance, will be deboned by your waiter with a flourish, right at the table.

The rest of the menu offers a nice selection of steaks and seafood, and there is a well-stocked salad bar from which you help yourself while awaiting the main course.

Even without the special mood created by the river, the low-ceilinged dining room is a delight, finished in dark wood and highlighted by old-style, stained-glass hanging lamps and all sorts of mementos, maps, and pictures of the woods and mountains. Off to the side is a similarly furnished little bar, a popular place indeed in the evening when a local guitar player comes in to sing old hits on demand from the audience. There always seem to be more people around the dining room and bar at night than can possibly stay at the lodge, so it is obvious that many of them come all the way from Yakima, the nearest town, for dinner and an evening out. Such an observation speaks volumes about Whistlin' Jack's quality and attractiveness.

During the day the restaurant is always open for breakfast and lunch. Anyone who missed the trout at dinner can have a fisherman's trout breakfast instead!

Timberline Lodge

Distances:

From Portland—65 miles; allow 2 hours

From Seattle—240 miles; allow 5 hours

From Vancouver, B.C.—385 miles; allow 8 hours

Features:

Huge, stone and timber lodge at timberline on Mount Hood; superb views, fresh air, comfortable accommodations; fascinating history; easy access from Portland

Activities:

Alpine and cross-country skiing, climbing and hiking, swimming, saunas, aprés-ski activities in bar

Seasons:

Year-round, including summer skiing on permanent snowfield

Rates:

$38 to $75 for two people in a private room; $26 for two people in a bunk room

Address:

Government Camp, Oregon 97208

Phone:

(503) 231-5400; toll free in Washington, 1-800-457-1406; toll free in Oregon, 1-800-452-1335

Spring scene at Timberline Lodge

To the uninitiated, it is a strange sight on a balmy summer day to see the parade of ski-laden cars, some convertibles with tops down, headed up through the national forest to Mount Hood. But the strange phenomenon is easily explained because the destination is Timberline, which offers some of the finest spring and summer skiing in the Pacific Northwest. When all other areas shut down for the season, Timberline can continue to provide good skiing because of the permanent snowfield that is so high it never melts.

The hub of activity here is the cavernous lodge, which exudes an aura of history that makes it a fascinating place for all kinds of travelers—not just skiers. Designated a historic landmark, Timberline is like a romantic castle, yet was built by the Work Progress Administration in the midthirties during the depth of the Great Depression. In just two years an army of workers, trucked up each day from temporary barracks at Government Camp, built this massive edifice from stone quarried from the surrounding hills and timber cut from the native forest. The six huge hexagonal main columns, each originally a single tree trunk, were shaped by hand at the site. An impressive stone fireplace with six openings was built to rise through three stories in the core of the lodge and was adorned with six great curled pairs of andirons shaped from railroad track by blacksmiths. Local craftsmen and artists filled the lodge with handcrafted furniture, wood carvings, paintings, sculptures, mosaics, and woven rugs and drapes.

The vast undertaking was one of Franklin Roosevelt's most cherished projects, and upon its completion he traveled to Oregon in 1937 to dedicate it personally. Guests of the lodge can see the whole story of the remarkable endeavor and Roosevelt's involvement in it in a captivating twenty-minute film that is often shown in the lobby after dinner to anyone who wants to see it.

Routes and Distances

From Portland take U.S. 26 east to Government Camp, a distance of sixty miles. Slightly beyond the Government Camp ski area and commercial activity, a large marker indicates the Timberline turnoff on the left. Drive approximately five miles up this steep road to the lodge. Chains may be necessary in winter.

Accommodations

All overnight accommodations at Timberline are in the lodge itself. A separate wing is maintained for conventions; the rest of the facility is used by skiers and tourists. Besides seven dormitories with bunks for skiers, the lodge has fifty-three individual rooms, most of which are designated "economy" or "standard." The economy units are small but comfortably furnished with twin beds or a double bed and a private bath. The standard room has much the same floor plan but is a bit larger. In addition to these two basic types, there are some larger, airier corner rooms and several spacious deluxe units (including the one occupied by Roosevelt himself), restored to their original gracious state. Seven rooms have their own fireplaces.

Timberline has an eighty percent annual occupancy, with weekends booked almost solidly throughout the winter ski season; even weekdays are often booked a couple of weeks in advance. Summers, though, are more open, and April and May are the slowest months of the year.

A word of warning to summer visitors: the temperature on Mount Hood at the high level of timberline can change from ninety degrees Fahrenheit to below freezing in a matter of hours. Come prepared with both winter and summer gear.

Activities

Alpine skiing is the number one activity at Timberline. The lifts run right beside the lodge so that no hiking in clumsy ski boots is necessary. In summer, only the upper lift on the permanent snowfield is usable; at all other times skiers buckle up at the front door and start down, coming back up on a chair that discharges next to the lodge, where they transfer to second and third lifts going up into the treeless slopes above. From the top, it

Sunny day of skiing at Timberline

is possible to make a single uninterrupted run of five full miles, all the way to Government Camp and the highway below. Cross-country skiers range out on the open side hills or follow a marked trail to Government Camp at the bottom.

Mount Hood is also one of the most popular mountains in North America for climbers. They start at the lodge at earliest light in order to make the ascent before the sun softens the snow. Climbing time varies with weather conditions but is normally nine to ten hours for inexperienced climbers. Ice axes, crampons, and summit packs can be rented at the lodge's ski shop, which will also put together climbing parties and provide skilled climbing leaders to serve as guides and instructors.

After a day of skiing or climbing or simply watching, many guests take advantage of the outdoor pool at the west end of the lodge. It is a spectacular experience to relax in clear, eighty-six degree water with snowbanks all around and the great white mountain looming above. And it is all the more exciting if the weather is bad and snow is swirling down. After the swim you can slip into the saunas next to the pool for a final touch of warmth.

Those who hate to quit can ski on into the evening, when lights illuminate the slopes at Timberline. The pool, too, is open until eleven in the evening.

After skiing and swimming the center of activity moves to the Ram's Head Bar. Window tables overlook the lifts going up the mountain on one side and people skiing down the slope on the other side. Skiers who have had enough can rest in comfort while watching others work the slopes or they can sing and laugh and make new friends in traditional aprés-ski fashion.

Things change a great deal in late spring and summer. Skiers still ski, but many more people come to enjoy the mountain scenery and its unique ecology. Wildflowers and mushrooms make their appearance late at these elevations, but they come in startling abundance, and hikers fan out over the trails to take photographs and hunt for rare specimens and to take in the spectacular views.

Dining

The main dining area is the Cascade Room, where the lodge's decor is carried through perfectly in the heavy-beamed ceiling, paneled walls, hard-

Skier at the lodge

wood plank floors, and beautiful view windows. Massive ornamental wrought-iron gates weighing a ton apiece open at mealtimes, and guests are invited into the cheerful room, where a fire always glows in the massive fireplace.

Like so many things here, even the menus have historic significance: they are exact replicas of the original 1937 silk-screened menu for the banquet celebrating the Roosevelt dedication. Equally innovative are the entrées, created by a young chef who is highly praised in these parts and encompassing a wide variety of selections, including rabbit, duckling, bouillabaisse, and a curried shrimp, pork, and vegetable quiche, as well as the standard steak and fish items. Add to this a fine wine list and good desserts, and a delightful meal is a surety.

The Cascade Room is open for breakfast and lunch, and there is also a skiers' deli in the lower level of the lodge for short-order service.

South
Getaways

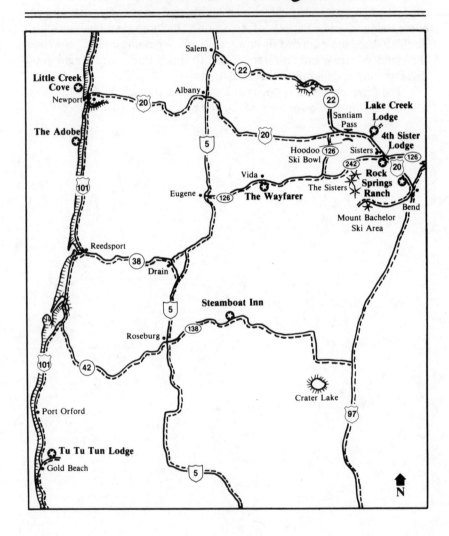

Tu Tu Tun Lodge

Distances:
From Portland—310 miles; allow 6½ hours
From Seattle—485 miles; allow 10 hours
From Vancouver, B.C.—630 miles; allow 13 hours

Features:
An elegant "fishing camp" for those who like to fish in style; for nonfishermen, a riverside resort with class, comfort, and a convivial atmosphere, located on the Rogue River

Activities:
Steelhead and salmon fishing, wild-water boat trips, swimming, pitch-and-putt golf, sight-seeing, hiking, nature watching; golf nearby

Seasons:
April through November, with special openings in winter when there are prime fishing conditions

Rates:
$57 for two people

Address:
Route 1, Box 365, Gold Beach, Oregon 97444

Phone:
(503) 247-6664

Approach to Tu Tu Tun Lodge

Tu Tu Tun, as one might expect, is an Indian name taken from a tribe whose encampment once occupied the lodge site. History records that the tribe was a happy people whose livelihood came easily from the river and ocean beaches; food was plentiful and life was good. Today, Tu Tu Tun Lodge is characterized by low-keyed elegance, immaculate maintenance, and most importantly, the extraordinary hospitality of its two young owners, Dirk and Laurie Van Zante.

The big, comfortable lodge, with its dining room and bar, fireplace and inviting living room, is of relatively new construction, situated to overlook a broad sweep of the Rogue River. It is a place of great quiet; there is little traffic on the road, no telephones, and no television. Deer are often seen just outside the rooms, browsing in the orchard between the buildings and the road.

The clientele at Tu Tu Tun is cosmopolitan, with guests from many states and many walks of life, and the Van Zantes' contagious friendliness quickly makes the newest arrivals feel at home and included in the group. Everyone gathers by the fireplace before dinner, and then they eat together family style at eight-place dining tables.

All during one's stay, no money changes hands and no tabs are signed or exchanged. At check-out time, one bill takes care of everything, including tips, boat fares, and whatever incidentals have been incurred. It is a final gracious touch that somehow the management has unobtrusively kept track in order to avoid all appearances of mundane commercialism.

Routes and Distances

Located at Gold Beach, Tu Tu Tun is a long way—the whole length of Oregon—from the closest big city, but that seems to be no deterrent to those who like the place, because they just keep coming back. The location midway between the population centers of California and the Northwest makes it especially attractive as a stopover for those traveling the coast, and it is not unusual for people to go out of their way to allow extra days for a visit whenever they make the trip.

Coming from the north, some like to drive the whole way on U.S. 101 just for the scenery, but the fastest route is to take Interstate 5 south from Portland. About six miles below Cottage Grove look for signs announcing the turnoff to Drain on Oregon 38, and follow 38 through Drain and across the Coast Range to Reedsport. From Reedsport take 101 to Gold Beach, but just before crossing the Rogue River into town turn left on the North River Road. Follow this for six miles to Tu Tu Tun Lodge on the right. From Port Orford on, spectacular scenery at every new bend in the road makes this drive a special pleasure.

Accommodations

Guest quarters are in a separate two-story building adjacent to the lodge. There are sixteen units, each with a view of the river and a little deck from which to enjoy it. All rooms have identical floor plans with a dressing area, a bath, and a bedroom with two double beds. Even though the rooms seem casual because of their knotty pine ceilings and the rustic fishing paraphernalia used for decor, they have a touch of elegance. For example, guests arrive to find a bouquet of fresh flowers in the bedroom and another in the bath, as well as up-to-date magazines selected to suit the tastes of both men and women.

An original home behind the orchard is now known as the Garden House and is the only other accommodation. It has been renovated to make comfortable quarters for a large family or for two or three couples traveling together. Since it has a complete kitchen, it is an ideal head-quarters for groups of winter steelheaders because they can use it when the main lodge and its dining room are closed. Special arrangements can be made with the management for its use in the off-season.

Activities

All Oregon's rivers have distinct characteristics, and they are fished accordingly. On the McKenzie, people work from a drifting oar-powered boat. On the Umpqua, they wade and fight the current on slippery footing while fly casting. On the Rogue, though, they fish every way, from bank or boat or wading, depending on the season and what they are after. It yields spring-run Chinook from April through June, summer steelhead from August through November, and fall Chinook and silvers in August

Passengers board jet-boat for Rogue River trip

and September. And for any of these, Tu Tu Tun Lodge is as fine an operating base as a serious fisherman could want. The host, Dirk Van Zante, has a keen knowledge of the river; depending on his guests' experience and desires, he steers them to the right guide, or draws maps of the river showing where the action is and how to get there, and helps line up needed boats and gear.

But although fishing is the preeminent activity, it would be a shame to visit lower Oregon without taking the wild-river trip up the Rogue. Jerry's Jet Boats, which start at Gold Beach, come by the Tu Tu Tun dock to pick up passengers each morning. Breakfast at the lodge is at eight and the boats stop at half-past eight, so guests get their gear together, have breakfast in the dining room, and walk directly to the dock. The jet boat goes fifty-two miles, as far as physically possible, into the wild heartland of the Rogue. Even skeptics who dislike organized tours come back and endorse this educational and thrilling experience. The boats are of shallow draft, powered by two maneuverable jets. The trip consists of fast dashes between points of interest, with stops to watch otters, deer, eagles, bear, herons, ospreys, and other creatures from close up as well as to admire waterfalls and geological formations. The pilot explains the river's history as he goes. At midmorning there is a rest stop for coffee and leg stretching, and at noon at isolated Paradise Lodge, there is a two-hour lunch stop, which allows time to hike a little way and sample the famous Rogue River Trail on which you will probably meet backpackers making the three-day trip across the Klamath Range from the vicinity of Grants Pass.

Downriver the trip is much faster. The boat skims the water's surface at high speed, sliding delicately around bends, skipping over rapids, and nimbly avoiding rocks and shoals much like a slalom skier flying downhill. It is an exciting journey, but be advised that the weather in the back-country can change dramatically and unexpectedly, so take a windbreaker and layers of warm clothes as protection against the wind and cold, as well as a hat and sunglasses should it turn hot instead.

Back at the lodge after the boat trip there is just time before dinner for a dip in the heated pool, which is long and narrow and good for doing laps. After dinner on long summer evenings it is still light enough to try the little pitch-and-putt course in the orchard between the Garden House and the guest quarters. If you shoo the deer off, you can practice there all you want. For serious golf, the nine-hole Cedar Bend course with lush fairways and greens is eight miles away on the Highway 101 cut-off road.

If a hike is in order, visit the canyon just across the road from the lodge, or ask Dirk for directions to get on one of the more adventurous trails in the area.

Kayakers on Rogue River

Patio overlooks pool and river at Tu Tu Tun

Dining

Dinner is a congenial time at Tu Tu Tun. At half-past six an old school bell sounds a half-hour warning and invites guests to congregate around the big fireplace in the lodge to have cocktails and get acquainted. The hosts unobtrusively introduce and mix people and, when the time arrives for dinner, seat them at the large round tables in the dining room, shipboard style, according to who might most enjoy each other. There is no menu; the same meal is served to all. Each table has a lazy Susan on which the courses are laid out, and guests help themselves as it revolves. Homemade soup comes first, then salad and homemade bread. The main course might be baked Chinook salmon, fresh from the river, or thick slices of prime rib with crisp zucchini. Whatever it is, it will be excellent, and there is a small, select wine list for those who like wine with dinner.

Guests are equally spoiled at breakfast, with selections of eggs, fruit, homemade biscuits, or fluffy hot cakes with hot maple syrup. Lunch is available for anyone remaining at the lodge, and box lunches are prepared ahead for those going boating, fishing, or picnicking.

For those who want some variety, there are two good seafood restaurants in Gold Beach: the Captain's Table along U.S. 101 on the south side of town and the Nor'wester near the river mouth in the port area.

Little Creek Cove

Distances:
> From Portland—139 miles; allow 2¾ hours
> From Seattle—314 miles; allow 6½ hours
> From Vancouver, B.C.—459 miles; allow 10 hours

Features:
> Spacious, tastefully furnished condominium units built astride a stream on an ocean beach; secluded location with impressive views; all units have fully equipped kitchens; no organized sport facilities

Activities:
> Beach activities, golf nearby, sight-seeing, shop and gallery browsing

Seasons:
> Year-round

Rates:
> $42 to $55 plus 5% city tax for two people

Address:
> 3641 Northwest Ocean View Drive, Newport, Oregon 97365

Phone:
> (503) 265-8587

Condominium units astride stream at Little Creek Cove

Besides the beach itself, the main feature of Little Creek Cove is its buildings. Fine examples of first-rate Northwest architecture, they are designed to take advantage of the natural attributes of the beach and surrounding landscape. For example, a clear little stream flows through the property. It could have been channeled into a culvert, but instead the buildings were set on piling to permit the stream to flow unimpeded beneath them down to the sea. The bonus is that the tall foundations help the sumptuously comfortable apartments above to have better views. There are thirty-two of these luxury units, most of which are kept by their individual owners in a rental pool. Professional managers who live on the site handle reservations and maintenance.

Little Creek is a hideaway in every sense of the word. Couples who come with their own supplies can be completely alone with the beach and its fascinations and never go into town, if that is what they want. Many guests come as foursomes in order to devote themselves to golf in the morning, beachcombing in the afternoon, and bridge in front of the fire in the evenings. In either case, in this quiet place they can enjoy the assurance that there will be no interruptions or distractions from outside their own group to spoil the tranquility of their visit.

Nevertheless, should a bit of outside entertainment be desirable, Newport with its many attractions is just to the south, and the Oregon coast's famed "twenty miracle miles" stretch to the north. Opportunities for every kind of adventure are thus available for the choosing, with Little Creek Cove strategically located in the center of it all.

Routes and Distances

Little Creek Cove is north of Newport on the Ocean View Drive, just off U.S. 101, across from the Agate Beach Golf Course. Take either Oregon 18 from Portland to Lincoln City and then 101 south to Newport, or U.S. 20 from Albany-Corvallis west across the Coast Range, directly to Newport.

Accommodations

Beyond any question, the apartments at Little Creek are as spacious, tastefully furnished, and comfortable as any in the Northwest. No two are exactly alike, as each was furnished by its particular owner, but all are in accordance with standards established by the developers.

Three basic units are available. The smallest is the studio, which is a large living room with a full kitchen and bath. The sofa in these units unfolds to make a queen-size bed. Next in size are one-bedroom units exactly the same as the studios but with a large separate bedroom and a second

Decks overlook beach at Little Creek

bath or half-bath. The largest are two-bedroom units, also the same but with two bedrooms and two full baths. All of the units have individual outside entries, decks, fireplaces with wood and kindling supplied, and excellent exposure to the ocean.

Activities

Half the visitors to Little Creek bring their golf clubs in order to play Agate Beach Golf Course, just a few hundred yards north and across the highway from the condominiums. This is a nine-hole, par-thirty-eight course, pretty and meticulously maintained. Its modern clubhouse has a coffee shop and a well-equipped pro shop with carts, rentals, and a full-time teaching pro. Billing itself as "the sweetest course on the Oregon coast," it is regarded as challenging and fun to play.

Agate Beach itself is wide, flat, and very hard, making it ideal for walking and running. Most of the agates are found at the far ends of the beach where the sand gives way to stony areas. Occasionally, wave action will uncover pockets of gravel right in front of the condominiums, making good agate hunting; then the next tide is apt to cover them again. The underlying base of gravel explains why the beach here is so hard and also why it is not very good for clamming.

In winter and spring, typically high winds along this section send loose sand flying across the beach. The incessant blasting effect smooths

Golf course across road from Little Creek Cove

and molds individual pieces of driftwood among the jumbles lying above high water, with the result that searchers can find all sorts of unusual and attractive shapes to take home.

The town of Newport originally was concentrated along the waterfront area north and east of the big bridge over the Yaquina River. A fleet of commercial fishing boats berthed there, and a number of canneries and processing plants bordered the docks. Though the main part of town has since expanded to the north along the highway, the boats and canneries are still as active as ever along the original waterfront. Recently many of the buildings in this Old Town section, in between the canneries and docks, have been restored and are now occupied by restaurants, seafood markets, and arts and crafts shops. On a nice day it is fun to take a lazy stroll along the waterfront here, catching glimpses of the activity in the canneries and watching the fishing boats come and go and unload their fish. Make a point, if possible, to have a seafood lunch in one of the restaurants and look in on the shops and galleries.

Charter boats operate out of Newport and the Yaquina Bay Marina for deep-sea fishing expeditions. Since this is one of the Oregon coast's "hot spots" for this activity, guests of Little Creek Cove might want to arise early one morning and give this sport a try.

Dining

Since every unit here has its own complete kitchen with all necessary utensils and flatware, it is not necessary to go out for meals. Many guests prefer to take advantage of the nearby seafood markets to cook and experiment with the many fresh-caught local delicacies, perhaps fixing dinner over a driftwood barbecue in the traditional beach-front manner.

There are, nevertheless, a number of good restaurants in the area. Mo's, on the waterfront, is at one end of the available spectrum. Everyone at Mo's sits on plain wooden benches at large common tables. There is no liquor, just good seafood and quick service in a convivial, super-informal atmosphere, and the prices are right. The sign confronting you when you enter says, "Don't just stand there. Crowd right in and join the confusion. Half the fun at Mo's is rubbing elbows with nice people from all over the world."

Quite the opposite is Amerik's, located in an old, elegantly remodeled house just below the south end of the big bridge at the first turnoff to the left. Dinner is served by reservation only and is chosen from an extensive menu of elaborately prepared gourmet dishes. Prices are appropriately high, but the place is always crowded, attesting to its popularity.

A good place in between the informal and the elegant is the Town House, on the highway a short distance north of Little Creek Cove. Another is Gracie's Sea Hag Restaurant, where you are guaranteed "the best clam chowder on the coast,'' and usually a good time to boot. It is in Depoe Bay, eleven miles north of Little Creek.

Steamboat Inn

Distances:

From Portland—227 miles; allow 4½ hours

From Seattle—402 miles; allow 8 to 9 hours

From Vancouver, B.C.—550 miles; allow 11 to 13 hours

Features:

Small, very unusual fisherman's inn in a remote location on the North Umpqua River; particularly notable for extraordinary dining and personal attention to guests

Activities:

Fly-fishing for steelhead and trout, sunbathing, hiking, picnicking, swimming, river watching

Seasons:

Ostensibly operates year-round, but January through March is very slow and sometimes the inn closes; May through July is always full as it's the top fishing season; September and October are prettiest months and a good time for a visit

Rates:

$34 for two people; $12 for each additional adult; no extra charge for children

Address:

Toketee Route, Box 36, Idleyld Park, OR 97447

Phone:

(503) 496-3495 or (503) 498-2411

Roadside view of Steamboat Inn

It is difficult to describe the appeal of Steamboat Inn because its rough-hewn charm is so thoroughly intertwined with its owners and managers, Jim and Sharon Van Loan. Their motto is "You are a stranger here but once," and they mean it. Enormous pains are taken to treat each visitor in a personal and friendly way so that guests will remember the trip as a warm and companionable experience.

At first sight the inn looks small and unprepossessing, more like a quiet country store with its two small gas pumps out in front. It soon becomes apparent, however, just how essential those gas pumps are; Steamboat is the only place on eighty miles of backwoods highway where loggers, truckers, and local people can stop to fill up and enjoy a cup of coffee.

Step inside the inn and you are in a room that serves as lobby, dining room, lunch counter, and emporium for fly-fishing supplies. This room, with its dark wood paneling and large stone fireplace, takes a few minutes to explore. The ceiling is lined with rows of fly rods suspended from hooks, the shelf on the back wall is loaded with boxes of line, leaders, and reels, and a cabinet with fifty or so little drawers contains all the special flies presumably favored by Umpqua steelhead. Other walls are adorned with photos of famous local fishermen at work, and racks of fishing magazines and almanacs plus a giant wine rack that suggests good things to come. The long tables in the middle of the room are made of great slabs of pine with well-rounded corners polished by what must have been generations of constant use.

The traditions of Steamboat Inn go back to the early 1930s, when a fisherman named Clarence Gordon built the old North Umpqua Lodge across the river. It became the mecca of many fishermen, including the famous author Zane Grey. In the fifties Gordon· moved to the present site and changed the name to Steamboat Inn. This unusual name, incidentally, comes from the jargon of old-time miners who referred to slickers who sold false claims and then promptly left town on the next boat as "steamboaters." The inn changed hands only once before the Van Loans purchased it in 1975 and began to dedicate themselves to maintaining and improving the atmosphere and traditions of the past.

Routes and Distances

There is no trick to finding Steamboat. Drive to Roseburg on Interstate 5 and take Oregon 138 east toward Crater Lake. The first sixteen miles on 138 is a wide freeway through farming and logging country, then suddenly the road narrows to two lanes, signs of civilization disappear, and the traveler enjoys twenty-four miles of the most scenic driving imaginable. The road closely follows the roiling North Umpqua, where majestic old-growth timber covers the banks on both sides. Traffic is generally light, and there are no power or telephone lines to desecrate the views. Forty-five minutes from Roseburg you arrive at Steamboat Inn, which is easily found on the right side of the road.

Large deck overlooking the river at Steamboat

Accommodations

The six small guest cabins at Steamboat are set along the edge of a high bank of the river. They are furnished rather simply, but they provide the necessities for a comfortable stay. The interiors are finished in knotty pine, and each cabin has two double beds, a chest of drawers, a couple of chairs, and a bath with shower and a more than generous supply of towels. What the cabins might lack in glamour is compensated by the large, pleasant veranda that runs along the river side of the cabins, joining them together in a wide promenade. A quiet corner can be found for reading or contemplation, but for those in an expansive mood the veranda provides ample opportunities for socializing or perhaps sharing a cocktail hour.

Activities

The North Umpqua is known as one of the most difficult North American rivers to fish. It is also one of the few rivers with summer-run steelhead, the royalty fish of the Pacific coast. No boats are allowed on the North Umpqua, and for fifteen miles in each direction from Steamboat no bait or spinners are permissible. Only fly-fishing is allowed, and all of these conditions create the challenge that brings the most skillful of fishermen back to this river year after year and generation after generation.

The river is fished by wading, and the difficulty stems from its powerful current and tricky bottom, which must be negotiated to approach the holes where the fish lurk. Each of these holes has a name, such as Fighting Hole, Secret Pool, Sawtooth, and the Upper and Lower Mott. Since the old-timers all have their favorites, they tend to rise very early in the morning to be sure to be first at their particular spot.

While the fishermen are out on the river, the nonfishing visitors at Steamboat like to sit on the quiet veranda overlooking the river and daydream or read. It is an unimaginably peaceful place to be. Tiring of that, they hike and picnic on the fishing trails along the water's edge or on the more challenging trails into the scenic high country. In summer, they sun on the flat rocks leading down to the river just below the inn or go up Steamboat Creek to swim in its clear pools.

Dining

All day long at Steamboat meals and snacks are served to whomever might drop in, but dinner is a different matter. Every evening during the fishing season and on weekends the rest of the year, a justly famed "fisherman's dinner" is served a half hour after sundown, but only to those with reservations. About fifty dinner guests can be accommodated, and they all congregate at the appointed hour because dinner is served only once and a common menu is served to all.

When the guests are assembled, the blinds are drawn, a "Closed for

Steelheader tries his luck on North Umpqua

View of the river from Steamboat Inn

the Evening'' sign is hung outside, and the fisherman's dinner begins, first with a social period when aperitifs and hors d'oeuvres are served and everyone mills around getting acquainted. Fly-fishermen may tend to be loners on the river, but when the day's action is over they become gregarious indeed and need no invitation to swap yarns and stories until it is time to sit down to eat.

The big slab table in the middle of the room seats at least twenty, and the rest of the guests are grouped around similar tables built on a smaller scale. Dinner is served by candlelight, with numerous carafes of wine, which are included in the dinner, already set out on the tables. Sharon Van Loan is a gourmet-meal planner with style and imagination, and the food each night consists of one of her inspirations accompanied by a pretty salad, homemade bread, and desserts, all seeming even more elegant because of the rustic surroundings and isolated location.

On many nights talented local people supply entertainment, often spontaneously. It also is not unusual, as the evening wears on, for the guests to pick up the spirit and sing old songs together until the early-rising fishermen begin to drift off for a night's dreaming of the big one they plan to hook the next day.

The Wayfarer

Distances:

From Portland—139 miles; allow 3 hours
From Seattle—314 miles; allow 7 hours
From Vancouver, B.C.—462 miles; allow 10 hours

Features:

Picture-pretty cabins hidden on the banks of a brook in an Oregon forest; all units have fireplaces and are spacious, arranged for privacy, and impeccably maintained and furnished

Activities:

Trout and steelhead fishing, white-water inner-tubing, tennis, golf, lawn games, hiking

Seasons:

April through September; other times by special arrangement

Rates:

$37 to $46 for two people, $44 to $80 for families

Address:

Star Route, Vida, Oregon 97488

Phone:

(503) 896-3613

Cabin on river's edge at the Wayfarer

Located on the McKenzie River, deep in one of the loveliest forest areas in the Northwest, the Wayfarer resort is delightful in every detail, but is not yet well known and therefore all the more a discovery.

There are other resorts with nice accommodations dotting the banks of this beautiful river, and some are in equally picturesque settings under their canopies of mossy trees on the water's edge. What is it then that makes the Wayfarer especially appealing? The answer is in the many small details that add up to a great deal of charm. Not every resort has fresh cut flowers, a bowl of filberts picked on the property, and a fire already laid in the fireplace in your room when you arrive. Nor does everyone have a trout-stocked pond set aside just for little fishermen too young for the river. Nor do they have an old-fashioned swimming hole or a fine tennis court and owners who can easily be persuaded to drop everything for a game of mixed doubles with their guests.

It is, in fact, the careful personal attention that owners Terry and Pat Patton give to every detail of the operation that renders the Wayfarer the quintessence of charm and good taste. Originally from California, this couple came to the Wayfarer for years as guests, but they so loved the place that when the opportunity presented itself, they jumped at the chance to buy it and suddenly found themselves deeply committed to the resort business. Their fresh ideas and unflagging enthusiasm have produced one of Oregon's finest hideaways, one that in the years ahead is likely to become a standard of comparison that other resorts will have to strive to match.

Routes and Distances

The Wayfarer experience begins when you cross the McKenzie River over one of Oregon's historic covered bridges at the little town of Vida. Vida is twenty-five miles east of Eugene on Oregon 126. Cross the bridge and drive four miles south along the river to where the Wayfarer's distinctive sign, with its straw hat and fishing rod, is seen on the left.

Accommodations

Nine of the eleven cabins at the Wayfarer are scattered on the bank of Martin Creek just above the point of confluence with the McKenzie. They vary in size, but all harmonize with the surroundings and each has its own individual charm and orientation.

There are two small studio cabins and one very large cabin with four bedrooms and two and a half baths (excellent for a big family gathering); all of the others are one- or two-bedroom units. For couples a studio is adequate, but for just a slightly higher rate a one-bedroom cabin has the additional value of a large separate living area and a deck overlooking the river. The cabins with two bedrooms and two baths make economical accommodations for two couples traveling together.

The cabins all have slightly different exposures: some with sunny decks that are delightful in spring and others with shady decks that are appreciated as summer wears on. Two of the cabins overlook the swimming hole, and two others have a close view of a big rock where fascinating birds called "teeter birds," do a strange dance before diving into the water in search of food. Other cabins look out across the stream into the mossy forest.

Each cabin is equipped with cable television, a fireplace, and a fully

Cabin on edge of spacious lawn

equipped, modern kitchen. A public telephone is centrally located at the resort, and there is also a laundry room on the premises.

Activities

Oregon has many good trout streams, but few surpass the McKenzie for either beauty or production of fish. This is a favorite stream for fly casting. It can be fished either from the bank or from a boat, but a boat is best because entangling tree branches can be avoided and holes on both sides can be fished to advantage from the center of the stream. In fact, the famous "McKenzie River boat" was invented for use on this river, and the very best way to fish it is to hire a licensed guide who supplies the boat and tackle, handles the oars, and knows where to go and what lures to use. A day's trip costs about one hundred dollars for two fishermen; one fly-casts and the other trolls. For those who are unfamiliar with the art of fly casting, a day on the McKenzie is a valuable learning experience because the guides will teach as they go. At noon the practice is to stop along the riverbank for lunch, often frying some of the trout caught that very morning. The guide does the cooking and brings everything that is needed. The owners of the Wayfarer know who the best guides are and can make all the arrangements for a day on the river for their guests.

Sitting on the deck of your cabin watching the stream and the woods and forgetting the cares of the world hardly qualifies as an "activity." Nevertheless, it is the favorite pastime for those who are not out on the stream fishing—except, that is, for the tennis players, who have a fine, new, tournament-quality Laykold court waiting for their exclusive use.

Children find a lot to do in Martin Creek, where a temporary dam is built each year to form a swimming hole. Farther upstream, they like to inner-tube down on the current. Out on the McKenzie itself, some of the more adventuresome adults try inner-tubing in real rapids.

Horseshoes, outdoor Ping-Pong, and badminton are available at the resort. There is also the trout pond in which children under ten can learn the fun of fishing. Strolling the river banks is always popular, and for serious hikers there are good trails, such as the McKenzie River National Recreation Trail, in the surrounding national forest.

Finally, less than a half hour's drive upriver is the well-known and beautiful Tokatee Golf Course, one that no dedicated golfer would want

One on the line for McKenzie River fisherman

Historic covered bridge over McKenzie River

to miss.

Dining

For meals everyone is on their own at the Wayfarer, since there is no lodge or dining room, but this is no hardship, because each unit has its own fine kitchen. There is also a barbecue with an electric starter on every deck so all guests need to remember to bring is some charcoal. Once prepared, meals can be enjoyed on the deck in the complete privacy of a sylvan landscape.

If, on the other hand, it would be more convenient to have dinner out, Nona Lena's Riverside Inn, just across the covered bridge in Vida, is only a short drive away and is an exceptionally good restaurant. When looking for it, do not be misled by the multitude of name signs, all different and prominently displayed. Apparently the restaurant has changed hands a few times in the past, and the present manager has left all the old signs up because he doesn't want to lose any business built by former owners. You can enjoy a good steak or seafood dinner at Nona Lena's in front of a big friendly fireplace. For a real show after dinner, order a "Spanish Coffee"—the waiter will make it for you at tableside with a great flourish of flaming brandies, sugar and liqueurs from his well-stocked cart.

The Adobe

Distances:
From Portland—163 miles; allow 3¼ hours
From Seattle—338 miles; allow 7 hours
From Vancouver, B.C.—483 miles; allow 10 hours

Features:
Long-established, full-service seaside resort on a rocky coast where spectacular surf action is the rule

Activities:
Ocean watching, beach walking, marine-specimen collecting, fishing, scenic drives, sunbathing, picnicking

Seasons:
Year-round; generally well booked on weekends and in summer

Rates:
$33 to $40 for two people

Address:
P.O. Box 219, Yachats, Oregon 97498

Phone:
(503) 547-3141

Adobe Inn on Oregon coast

Ocean waves breaking against the rocks just yards from your bedroom window is the number one attraction of this resort, located between U.S. 101 and the Pacific. A long drive through a wide sweep of lawn bordered by wind-bent native pines brings you to the resort buildings, which are swept-wing shaped to conform to the line of the shore. A modern two-story addition has recently been incorporated into the complex, but the original structures are low lying, hunkered down against the storms, and built of adobe bricks made on the site from local earth. Adobe is seldom used outside the dry Southwest, and it is therefore a surprise to discover how well these heavy bricks can withstand the battering of wind and spray brought by winter's constant northwesters. But the bricks do powder on the outside, paint flakes, and anything made of metal corrodes quickly in this atmosphere. Maintenance is thus a constant battle at the Adobe, and a certain battered and rustic appearance, common to many structures built so close to the ocean, is hard to avoid.

Things are secure and cozy inside, however, and the inn is a well-known, long-time favorite of Oregonians, especially those from Eugene and Albany, who live barely two hours away. Many of them come back year after year at the same times, often asking for the one particular apartment that has the view they like best.

Routes and Distances

Yachats (pronounced "Ya-hots") is a tiny town of four hundred situated on the mid-Oregon coast at the point where the Yachats River runs into the sea. The Adobe Inn lies at Yachat's northern edge. From Portland drive west on Oregon 18 to U.S. 101 and then south along the coast to Yachats. Or go to Albany and take U.S. 20 over the Coast Range to Newport and then 101 south from there. The two routes are approximately equal in mileage, and both are easy drives through typically scenic Oregon backcountry.

Accommodations

The Adobe's thirty-eight rooms vary slightly in size and orientation, which accounts for a differing price schedule. Every room has an ocean view, however, and at least half have fireplaces, which are well worth requesting. Most of the rooms are furnished with comfortable king-size beds, and one of the delights of staying at the resort is being able to watch the surf in the morning—without even getting out of bed. All rooms have color television sets, wired to the cable, and for unknown reasons this section of coast has considerably better than average reception, something television buffs will appreciate.

In the original buildings the interior walls are the same heavy adobe brick as the exteriors, providing excellent soundproofing between rooms. The new wing has rooms that are a little more modern and spacious than those in the older section, but half of them are on a second floor and thus not quite so close to the waves. Covered parking areas are just outside the rooms, so moving in is easy and requires a minimum of luggage carrying.

Activities

Sojourning at the Adobe is not for those who need a lot of organized play to have a good time. In fact, when asked what those guests who come back so regularly do, the owner scratched his head, then replied, "They unwind." This doesn't mean there aren't things to do—far from it. But the emphasis is on the less strenuous pursuits.

The beach in this part of Oregon is rocky, but between the rocks are sheltered sand pockets for sunning and picnicking, and the jutting rock formations make ideal places from which bait casters can work the surf for sea perch and bass.

A favorite pastime is strolling a grassy path that follows the low bank along the coast to the north. When the tide goes out, many little pools are left containing rich finds of anemones, starfish, and other surprises.

An exciting phenomenon in this area is the smelt run in mid-July, a seasonal occurrence seldom seen on other open beaches. When they are making their run, these little fish, considered a delicacy by many, can be scooped up by the hundred with a hand net. It is never hard to tell when a run is in progress because swarms of swooping gulls pinpoint where the fish are.

Large numbers of gray whales migrate past this area in winter and spring, and a few in summer, and because they swim very near the surf line they are often sighted from the beach. Even closer in, sea lions can often be seen fishing among the waves.

Yachats is situated in the center of some of Oregon's most interesting sight-seeing. There are places such as the Devil's Churn, Cook's Chasm,

Expansive ocean view from Cape Perpetua

Rocky beach in front of Adobe Inn

and Captain Cook Point to explore. One not to miss is the Cape Perpetua Lookout, just south of town. A road winds up through a national forest to the top of the cape, and from this high vantage point a breathtaking view of 150 miles of coast from Cape Foulweather to Cape Blanco, stretches out before your eyes. A short nature trail around this high bluff affords views in every direction and also provides markers that explain the plants and wildlife of the area. On a warm day this is an incomparable spot for a picnic.

Farther south but just a short drive from Yachats is Florence, where the mammoth sand dunes first appear. Those who are not faint hearted might enjoy a wild ride in a dune buggy at one of the concessions near town. Those who would rather climb and explore on foot might prefer Honeyman State Park, a beautiful entrance to the dunes a mile south of town.

Even if you usually avoid commercial exhibits, you should not miss the Sea Lion Caves, halfway between Yachats and Florence. These caves and the adjacent rocky ledges form the only natural mainland sea-lion rookery in the North Pacific. An elevator makes the 200-foot descent through solid rock to sea level, affording a fascinating close-up view of the big sea lions as they swim in the waves, bark, and clamber over the rocks.

North of Yachats, Newport offers more enjoyable possibilities, such as poking around the fishing wharves, going out on one of the charter boats for a day, or, at the very least, enjoying a leisurely lunch at the Embarcadero while watching the commercial fishing boats come and go in the harbor.

Dining

To gain a full 180-degree outlook of the spectacular view, the Adobe dining room was built close to the beach in semicircular form. Even the dark beams on the ceiling are arranged in spoke fashion, pointing outward toward the sea. This is a delightful atmosphere in which to enjoy a slow dinner, particularly at sunset when the Pacific sky is putting on one of its spectacular shows.

A full menu is available, but the emphasis here is on seafood, particularly shellfish, fried in a light, delicate batter rather than prepared in sauces. These are done very nicely. A choice of soups and a green salad are served with all entrées, and a limited but representative wine list is available. As it grows dark, linger if possible and watch the flood-lit surf. Better still, order an after-dinner drink and take it upstairs to one of the tables in the "Crow's Nest" for a dramatic view of the ocean at night.

Breakfasts, including a special seafood breakfast, are served at the Adobe for several hours in the morning, but there is no lunch, probably because so many people take trips up and down the coast during the day. This is a good incentive to have picnic lunches at one of the many points of interest in the vicinity. Cape Perpetua should be high on the list: on a warm day when haze does not obscure the view it is an incomparable and memorable spot to eat. Yachats itself is another. The town is bordered by a wide sand beach along the estuary of the Yachats River, and right where it joins the ocean, forming an apex, is a little green park with trees and picnic tables—a fun place to spend an hour or two.

Rock Springs Ranch

Distances:
From Portland—174 miles; allow 3½ hours
From Seattle—349 miles; allow 6½ hours
From Vancouver, B.C.—494 miles; allow 10 hours

Features:
Working horse ranch combined with full modern resort activities, located in Central Oregon's high country; family-oriented summer program provides supervised activity program for children, freeing adults to pursue other interests

Activities:
Horseback riding, tennis, swimming, scenic hiking and touring; winter sports nearby

Seasons:
Year-round; one-week minimum stay, American plan, in summer season, 21 June through 21 September; two-day minimum stay in off-season

Rates:
$800 per week plus 6% service charge for two people in summer, includes all meals, horses, and many extras; $40 to $50 per day for two people in off-season, includes accommodations only

Address:
64201 Tyler Road, Bend, Oregon 97701

Phone:
(503) 382-1957

Guest cabin at Rock Springs Ranch

Donna Gill built Rock Springs Ranch in 1970, drawing on thirty-three years of experience in running guest ranches and managing girls' camps to design a family-oriented facility that would cater to all ages. She evolved a format that has found enthusiastic reception: essentially a one-price summer program with, as part of the package, full-time youth counselors to take full charge of children from after breakfast until bedtime. The children's activity program includes riding, swimming, games, and crafts, and they have their own dining room and even their own "cocktail hour" (fruit juice, of course). This leaves the adults, both those with and without young ones, to do what they want in company with other adults. If children are too small for such supervised activity, parents can bring their own babysitter, and Donna will provide him or her with free meals and lodging!

When you enter the ranch, you will immediately understand how it acquired its name. Behind the big, modern ranch house are a series of rock-rimmed, spring-fed lakes providing a cool, scenic backdrop to the main area of activity. Below the ranch house is the barn with its stables and corral, beside the lakes are the swimming pool and tennis courts, and up a slight rise are seven smaller buildings containing the living quarters. And to the north and west there is nothing but sagebrush, juniper, rimrock, and mountains as far as the most venturesome rider would care to go.

Routes and Distances

Seven miles northwest of Bend, Oregon, on U.S. 20 is the little town of Tumalo. Drive to Tumalo and look for the Tumalo Emporium on the west side of the road. A sign there shows the way to Rock Springs Ranch. Take the road past the Emporium, indicated by the sign, and follow more signs three miles to the ranch.

Accommodations

There are no rooms in the ranch house itself; all the living quarters are in the cottages just above the house. Most of these are divided into two full apartments that in turn can be divided in two, depending on the amount of space required. A full apartment, for example, has a big main room with a king-size bed or two twins, a lounge area, a fireplace, a complete kitchen with breakfast bar, and a bath. Double doors lead from this apartment into another bedroom, which also has either twin beds or a king, and its own bath. If separate parties use these two units, the connecting doors are simply locked. Since everyone pays the same price in the summer, the people with the kitchen half obviously have the better deal, but when you're busy with outside activities it doesn't make a great deal of difference. Donna Gill tries to assign the quarters according to her clients' preferences and needs.

In the winter season, when no common dining facilities are

Ranch house overlooks rock-rimmed lake

Fording the river on a trail ride at Rock Springs

available, it is necessary to have an apartment with a kitchen, so all rentals are made on that basis. At all times, the ranch house itself, with its big fireplace, living room, library, and little bar, provides a comfortable meeting place after skiing or a long ride or whatever activities occupied the day.

Activities

If there is anything horseback riders can get along without, it is fences dividing the countryside and confining their freedom of movement. Rock Springs Ranch is, therefore, a rider's paradise. Once outside its own gate, riders are in the Deschutes National Forest and can go, according to Donna Gill, "from Crater Lake to Mount Hood" without encountering a man-made obstruction. The ranch breeds and trains its own horses and maintains a string of about forty-five good saddle animals, with four wranglers to lead rides and teach horsemanship. All riding is part of the American plan in the summer season, so there are no extra charges and guests can ride as often as they desire. (In the off-season, when the package plan is not in effect, there is an hourly charge.) The corral and barn are a hundred yards from the main ranch house, and winter or summer, they are the focus of activity.

Adjacent to the ranch house, between the lakes, is a free-form pool heated by an array of solar panels. One segment of this divided pool is deep for adults, the other is shallow for young children; in either case, the pool is popular after a dusty time on the trail. Beyond the pool area are two hard-surfaced tennis courts with lights for night play.

As soon as the snow comes to Mount Bachelor, only thirty-two miles from the ranch, some of the emphasis at Rock Springs shifts from horses to skiing. Bachelor has seven chairs, three lodges, and a separate nordic center that keeps twenty miles of trails groomed for cross-country skiing.

Besides the opportunities provided for active sports, Central Oregon is particularly well endowed with scenic drives, unusual geological formations, parks and campgrounds, rivers, lakes, and mountains. The ranch house has a complete library of books, brochures, and other literature explaining where the points of interest are located and how you can best enjoy them.

Dining

In summer, when the American plan is in effect, meals in the ranch house are lavish and bountiful. Breakfast, lunch, and dinner are served buffet style, with something for everyone, whatever their particular tastes. Breakfasts are typical ranch fare with fruits and juices, bacon, ham or sausage, eggs, french toast or waffles: a good solid start for the day. Lunch also appeases the heartiest outdoorsman's appetite. Until the weather gets warm, the cook usually fixes hot casseroles and serves them with vegetables and fruits, but later in the summer the selection shifts to things such as taco salads and Crab Louies.

The highlight of the day is dinner, which is always preceded by a cocktail hour, usually on the ranch house's big outdoor deck. A little bar is available to supply ice and mixes, and guests bring their own liquor and wine or whatever they prefer. This is a time for relaxation, conversation, and getting acquainted with other people. Dinner itself is in the dining room and can always be counted on to offer more good food than most can eat. Because the American plan covers the cost of all meals, all summer nearly everyone eats in the ranch house. For a change of pace in summer, however, and by necessity in winter when the dining room is closed, guests can use their own kitchens in the living quarters, drive the seven miles into Bend, or go to the Emporium Restaurant at Tumalo. The Emporium is worth at least one meal, just for the experience. The decor is delightful—gay nineties throughout—the food is good, the service is friendly and efficient, and it is open all year.

4th Sister Lodge

Distances:

From Portland—156 miles; allow 3 hours
From Seattle—331 miles; allow 6½ hours
From Vancouver, B.C.—476 miles; allow 10 hours

Features:

Very spacious, comfortable condominium units quietly nestled in an Oregon pine grove; especially good value for two couples vacationing together; near interesting little town of Sisters; no restaurant

Activities:

Alpine and cross-country skiing and golf nearby; swimming, saunas, bicycling, browsing in shops and galleries, hiking and climbing

Seasons:

Year-round; major winter holidays and rodeo day in mid-June usually booked solid, otherwise availability is generally good, even on short notice; September and October are the most beautiful months

Rates:

$28 for two people for a bedroom and bath only, $40 for a complete one-bedroom apartment (for two couples together, average price is only $34)

Address:

P.O. Box 591, Sisters, Oregon 97759

Phone:

(503) 549-6441

Condominium units at 4th Sister Lodge

The 4th Sister Lodge is as fine a hideaway as anyone wanting comfort, quiet, and sunshine at a reasonable price could wish. It is a small, not well-known condominium development in which each unit is individually owned but kept in a rental pool when the owners are not using it themselves. The advantage of this system is its ability to provide vacationers with relatively luxurious accommodations compared with any but the most expensive commercial facilities.

The name "4th Sister" is derived from the commanding proximity of the Three Sisters mountain group looming as a backdrop to the west and also lending its name to the village lying across the small park from the condominiums.

Besides its luxurious accommodations the outstanding attribute of this lodge is its small, tucked-away nature. The green lawns, under a canopy of pines right in the middle of sagebrush country, create an oasislike atmosphere that invites laid-back relaxation. The dry, clean air, summer sunshine, winter snow, and central location in a rapidly growing resort area suggest that this will become an increasingly popular destination.

Routes and Distances
From Portland, take Interstate 5 to Salem and then Oregon 22 east

to where it merges with U.S. 20 just before Santiam Pass. Sisters is twenty-six miles beyond the merger point, and the 4th Sister Lodge is one block past the east edge of town, just off the highway and to the right. The latter part of this particular route is a memorable drive, passing through the heart of the southern Cascade Range and threading its way past such well-known peaks as Mount Jefferson, Three Fingered Jack, Mount Washington, and the Sisters themselves.

If the highway advisory should warn of snow clogging Santiam Pass in winter, take U.S. 26 from Portland to Madras. At Madras pick up U.S. 97 to Redmond. Turn west there on Oregon 126 to Sisters.

Accommodations

The 4th Sister has most of the same qualities that other Northwest vacation condominiums have except that these units are more spacious and more beautifully furnished, the rates are reasonable, and the availability is good.

The seven buildings have rough cedar siding with split-shake roofs and are arranged gracefully around the swimming pool in a wooded area that ensures privacy. Each condominium unit is a complete apartment with living room, lovely fireplace, kitchen, dining area, deck, washer-dryer, two bedrooms, and two baths. An entire unit is perfect for a family on a ski trip or a foursome on a bridge or golf outing. Otherwise the units are

Street scene in Sisters

the units are designed so they can be divided in two, with the living room–kitchen–bedroom combination as one rental and the second bedroom and bath as another. The second bedroom has its own small refrigerator and television set, making it quite comfortable and inexpensive for a couple just passing through. For no more than the cost of an average motel room, however, you can luxuriate in the larger section, which is the accommodation to choose whenever possible because of the fireplace, kitchen, and full living room.

Activities

More or less midway between two of Oregon's best known downhill areas, this is a dream location for skiers to establish "base camp." Hoodoo Bowl is the closest area, only twenty minutes away, and offers both day and night skiing. Mount Bachelor, famous for its dry powder and as a training base for U.S. ski teams, is forty-five minutes in the opposite direction. Really dedicated skiers can do Bachelor in the daytime, return to their lodge apartment for an early dinner in front of the fire, and then go night skiing at Hoodoo. Nordic skiers can strike out almost anywhere. The surrounding flat terrain is well suited to cross-country, while more challenging trails can be found throughout the nearby Deschutes National Forest and the Mount Washington Wilderness Area.

In summertime, the emphasis shifts largely to golf. Black Butte

Iron works shop in Sisters

Ranch, just a short drive away on the other side of Sisters, has two fine eighteen-hole links open for play from April through early November, depending on the weather. A complete pro shop and snack bar are available at the facility. Tee-time reservations are necessary on weekends and during summer's peak months; make arrangements by calling the golf shop at (503) 595-6689.

The same terrain that favors cross-country skiing in winter is good for bicycling in the warm months, and a lot of bicyclists, particularly tourists passing through loaded down with camp gear, are seen on the roads around Sisters. Bring your own bikes, however, as rentals are not available locally.

Tennis players are not so well favored. The lodge is thinking about buying adjacent property to build courts of its own, but at best that will be two years away. Meanwhile, players have to be content with the high school's two asphalt courts. The nets are made of steel fencing, and the asphalt has some bad spots, but the courts are close-by, just through the park next to the lodge and across the highway.

At the lodge itself, in the center of the complex, are a heated swimming pool and a clubhouse containing shower rooms, saunas for men and women, and Ping-Pong and billiard tables.

Everyone visiting the 4th Sister should devote some time to strolling around town, taking in the frontier village atmosphere and inspecting the

Sisters peak looms over llama farm

galleries, pottery shops, wrought-iron works, and other arts and crafts enterprises centered here.

For something unusual to talk about after the trip, walk out past the Petersons' llama ranch on the north edge of town. Over four hundred of these curious, friendly animals thrive here, far from their native home in the Andes. Perhaps the gorgeous mountain backdrop behind the pastures makes them feel at home.

Dining

With their own convenient, fully equipped kitchens and dining areas, guests at the 4th Sister have no need to go out for meals, but if they want to go anyway, there are some good alternatives. The town of Sisters has several informal places to eat. Papandrea's is especially well known—people come to town from far and wide to enjoy one of their famous pizzas with a glass of beer or wine. The Gallery Restaurant and Bar has full services for all meals and also, as its name suggests, serves as a showroom for Ray Eyerly's notable Western paintings. The Depot Deli is an ideal spot for lunch, especially in good weather when you can eat at the sidewalk tables.

For a more elegant dinner, make reservations in advance, dress up a bit, and drive out eight miles on U.S. 20 to Black Butte Ranch, which, in addition to its good food, is worthwhile to see for its ambitious design and pretty setting.

Lake Creek Lodge

Distances:

From Portland—148 miles; allow 3 hours

From Seattle—323 miles; allow 6½ hours

From Vancouver, B.C.—468 miles; allow 10 hours

Features:

Especially good for people with children, but just as much fun for those without; offers a taste of western living in ranch country, with much to do for the active but opportunity to lay back for those seeking rest

Activities:

Horseback riding, tennis, swimming, bicycling, fly-fishing, hiking, lawn games; alpine and cross-country skiing and golf nearby

Seasons:

The lodge is open all year, but operates on a complicated schedule, catering to different groups at different times; 1 July to mid-September is the family season, with a modified American plan (rates include dinners); in late spring and early fall the dining room is open, but meals are charged separately; 15 October to 15 May the dining room is closed, and guests fend for themselves for meals

Rates:

$62 to $72 for two people in the summer season, including dinner; about $25 to $42 (varying with the date) in spring, fall, and winter

Address:

Sisters, Oregon 97759

Phone:

(503) 595-6331

Main building at Lake Creek Lodge

Lake Creek Lodge has never advertised nor been promoted—for sixty years it has enjoyed all the recommendation it needs by word of mouth. Of course, one of the qualities that is usually necessary for a true hideaway is exactly such lack of publicity, with those who know it treating it as their "own private place," which they loyally come back to season after season. (Indeed, the management had some misgivings about being included in this book, but their pride in the resort argued against being left out of any listing of the Northwest's best.)

What makes Lake Creek Lodge so respected is the way it has incorporated so many critical vacation elements to ensure good times for everyone who participates. The facilities are as complete as anyone could desire. The accommodations are comfortable and private. The climate is usually ideal for outdoor activities, with much sun, little rain, cool evenings, and freedom from insects. For couples with children, what is particularly appealing are the many things that keep children safely occupied all day long so adults can pursue their own interests. The setting also is exceptional. A forested lawn is bisected by a small trout stream that was dammed to make the lake around which all activities center. To the west, forming a majestic backdrop for the lodge and its facilities, are some of Oregon's best-known snow-covered peaks, including Mount Washington, the North Sister, and Three Fingered Jack.

Routes and Distances

Drive south to Salem on Interstate 5 and turn east on Oregon 22 to Stayton. From there all the way to the destination is one of the nicest drives in Oregon, following mountain streams and the shores of beautiful Detroit Lake nearly the whole distance, with many glimpses of the Central Cascades' snow-capped mountain peaks. Fine picnic sites abound along the lake shore and river, so there are many good places to stop if you plan a picnic lunch en route.

At Santiam Junction, 22 merges with U.S. 20 and heads up over Santiam Pass, where Hoodoo Ski Bowl is located. Skiers might check the distance from here for future reference. About ten miles before Sisters, start looking for a sign designating a turnoff on the left to Camp Sherman and the Metolius River. Follow this road toward Camp Sherman for three miles. A very modest sign marks the entrance to Lake Creek Lodge on the right.

Accommodations

Lake Creek Lodge has two types of guest accommodations, "houses" and "cottages," each quite different. The "houses" are just that: small two-or three-bedroom houses that can take two to eight persons and have nicely furnished living rooms, single or double baths, full kitchens, porches, and, in some cases, fireplaces. The four rustic cottages are simpler, with just two plainly furnished bedrooms and a connecting bath between. They have no cooking facilities, though a small refrigerator on the front

Cabins face lake where guests fish and swim

porch provides ice and can hold picnic supplies. People do not spend much time inside, however, because this is the country for outdoor living, so in front of each house or cottage are tables, lawn chairs, and occasional chaise lounges that can be pulled into the sun or under the trees for shade to read, nap, or play cards.

Quite appropriately, the family-oriented resort welcomes well-behaved pets, for a nominal charge of one dollar per day.

Activities

Many dedicated fishermen throughout Oregon were first bitten by the fishing bug as youngsters at Lake Creek Lodge. Every year the lake and stream are restocked with fish and opened to children under twelve for fishing. The limit is three fish per day, and the kids do catch them, often with an anxious parent in the background trying to explain the fine points of the dry fly and thinking about fried trout for breakfast.

When not fishing, the kids splash in the water on inner tubes or float down the stream itself, and at night sometimes make pitch boats to sail, burning, across the dark water. The adults lounge beside the lake all day in the sun to read or watch the fishing, and in the evenings they congregate there for cocktails before going up to the lodge for dinner.

But, besides the activities around the lake, there are a dozen other things to do as well. After adequately instructing their young, the parents can go barely a mile away for their own fly-fishing on the respected Metolius River. A horseshoe pit, shuffleboard, swings, and lawn games

Horse corral at Lake Creek Lodge

are arranged beside the lake. The two tennis courts behind the houses have good hard surfaces, recently redone, and for golfers, the fine eighteen-hole course at Black Butte Ranch is only a short drive east on U.S. 20.

Hiking opportunities on the extensive network of Forest Service trails are practically limitless. A hike planned with a picnic destination at the turn-around point is a good way to spend a day. Guests can borrow the lodge's copy of *Sixty Hiking Trails in the Central Oregon Cascades* to get ideas about where to go. Or you can take to the trails on horseback. The Lake Creek Corral, one hundred yards down the road, has horses saddled and ready to go, either for trail rides or equestrian instruction.

Bicycling is particularly excellent in this area. The roads are flat and not too heavily traveled and make a fine way to see the countryside, but bring your own bike as rentals are not available in the vicinity.

In winter the snowfall is usually heavy and many of the Forest Service roads remain unplowed, making ideal trails for cross-country expeditioners who don't want to risk getting lost in the forest itself. Finally, Hoodoo Bowl, with some of the best downhill runs in Oregon, is only twenty minutes away.

Dining

Dinners at Lake Creek are always a pleasant experience but especially in the warm months, when dinner is part of the package and all the guests gather at the lodge at seven for a leisurely meal and a chance to get to know one another. When the weather permits, which is most of the time in this part of Central Oregon, the dining room moves outside onto a large wooden deck. Glass screens along the sides protect diners from occasional breezes, making the deck a perfect setting for an enjoyable evening.

Inside or out, the dinners are sumptuous, served buffet style so everyone can take whatever they want. A typical meal might begin with savory French onion soup and tossed green salad, followed by barbecued steak, Indian corn pudding, a fresh vegetable, and homemade bread, topped off with big red strawberries and cream for dessert. No cocktails are served by the lodge, but guests are welcome to bring their own bottle of wine with them to dinner.

Lunches are not served because most guests like to have the noon meal picnic style, either away on an expedition or in front of their quarters by the lake. Besides, the "Wrangler Breakfast," served from eight to ten in the morning, is enough to tide a lot of people over until dinner. There are all the usual choices of bacon, sausage, eggs, and hot cakes, but the favorite is fresh trout, of which there is usually an ample supply provided by the industrious young anglers who catch more than their own families can eat.

During spring and fall, dinner is served but is not included in the room rates. In winter, when there is not enough activity to justify keeping the dining room open, it is closed entirely. The guests, most of whom are skiers,

Buffet dinner on the deck at Lake Creek Lodge

have the choice of going out for meals or cooking for themselves in their own kitchens in the houses. (Since the cottages have no facilities for cooking, they are seldom rented in winter.) The two closest outside places to eat are a little café at Camp Sherman, a mile distant, or the elegant dining room at Black Butte Ranch, five miles away. There is also a small store at Camp Sherman that is well stocked with vacation necessities, such as picnic supplies, soft drinks, fishing gear, and wine and beer.

Information Sources

Weather Information
British Columbia
(604) 273-8331 Taped forecasts for Vancouver and vicinity
(604) 273-2345 Specific information for anywhere in
Canada
(604) 270-9371 Taped forecasts of marine conditions
(604) 273-2373 Taped reports of mountain conditions in
winter
Oregon
(503) 255-6660 Taped statewide forecasts
Washington
(206) 662-1111 Taped forecasts for Seattle and vicinity
(206) 285-3710 Taped statewide forecasts
(206) 627-0865 Taped statewide forecasts
(206) 357-3856 Taped forecasts for Olympia and vicinity
(509) 624-8905 Taped forecasts for Spokane and vicinity

Ferry Schedules and Information
British Columbia Ferry Corporation
Vancouver   (604) 669-1211
Victoria   (604) 386-3431
Nanaimo   (604) 753-1261
Seattle   (206) 682-6865
Washington State Ferries
Seattle   (206) 464-6400
Statewide toll free   1-800-542-0818 or 7052
Black Ball Ferry
Seattle   (206) 622-2222
Port Angeles   (206) 457-4491
Victoria   (604) 386-2202

Airlines
San Juan Airlines
    Seattle   (206) 625-9116
    Bellingham   (206) 734-8087
Chelan Airways
    Chelan   (509) 682-5555
Pacific Western Airlines
    Vancouver   (604) 684-6161
    Seattle   (206) 433-5088

Miscellaneous
Washington State Patrol, Seattle   (206) 455-7700
Oregon State Patrol, Portland   (503) 238-8434
Royal Canadian Mounted Police, Vancouver   (604) 732-4511
Automobile Association of America, Seattle
    Taped reports of highway and road
        conditions   (206) 292-5421
    General Information   (206) 292-5353
Automobile Association of America, Portland
    Taped reports of highway and weather
        conditions   (503) 222-6721
    Highway and weather conditions for specific areas
        not on the tape   (503) 222-6700
    General information   (503) 222-6734
British Columbia Department of Highways
    Taped reports of road conditions   (604) 277-0112
British Columbia Auto Club, Trip Planning
    Department   (604) 732-3911

Checklist

House
House key
Babysitter and dog-sitter
    arranged
Doors and windows locked
Furnace turned down
Water and electric lights
    turned off
Neighbor to take in mail and
    newspapers arranged

Packing
Casual clothes
Dinner clothes
Walking shoes
Bathing suits and robes
Toilet articles

Personal
Money and checkbook
Glasses and sunglasses
Reservation confirmations
Camera and film

Sports Equipment
Binoculars
Bicycles
Tennis gear
Golf gear
Fishing tackle
Clamming equipment
Rain gear
Skiing gear
Rucksack

Refreshments
Thermos of coffee
Breakfast ingredients
Beverages
Snacks

Auto
Extra set of car keys
Chains (in winter)
Full gas tank

Other Books from Pacific Search Press